To: K
I hope y
our Story. God Bless You!
Raina

BEYOND
the steps and stares

RAINA FUTRELL

TATE PUBLISHING, LLC

DEDICATION

This book is dedicated to:

~ Cody . . .
   for allowing me to tell the story of his life through my eyes . . .
~ Paul . . .
   for being such a dedicated dad . . .
~ Thunderbutt . . .
   the little Princess
~ Ma . . .
   who kept the angels circling Cody with her prayers . . .
~ Cuckie . . .
   the devoted aunt next door
~ The M's . . .
   with gratitude to Uncle Sonny for finding alternate ways of going
   hunting and fishing for Cody's sake . . .
~Ms. J
~Ol' Girl
~Rachel . . .
   who has brought so much love to Cody's life
~All of our family, friends, doctors, nurses, teachers, coaches, and
   many others . . .
~Most of all, thanks to God . . .
   Who showed up to rescue us with His presence in all of the above.

ACKNOWLEDGMENTS

An extra special word of gratitude is awarded here to the administration of the hospital where I work for allowing me time away from work to handle all the crises of the seventeen years since Cody's birth. My deep appreciation also goes to the staff of the Neonatal Intensive Care Unit there, for they have lived through it all with me as I have continued to supervise them throughout Cody's life. To Lynn and Sharon, my closest colleagues and two of my dearest friends, your loyalty, encouragement, and friendships have helped me to raise Cody and still remain emotionally intact.

I am deeply indebted to Patrice, who gave so kindly and unselfishly of her valuable time, encouragement, and advice. She was so patient and skillful with the preliminary editing of this work—while continuing to be my dear, faithful friend. An expression of gratitude is also written here to Barry, who gave expert advice and sincere encouragement throughout the task of completing this work.

I am appreciative to the Whites, who allowed me countless, peaceful hours of writing time, sitting in that swing down by one of the ponds on their beautiful farm and who warmed the hearts of my family and me while cheering me on in the writing of this book.

A passage of remembrance is written here for Tony, Ma's brother, who in the absence of my dad and the passing of Paul's dad, stepped in as a substitute grandfather. He and Cody loved one another and they clowned around together, doing things like putting change in the bottom of the water glass as the tip for a waitress who gave poor service. They told each other a lot of goofy jokes. Tony passed away when Cody was eight, but one of our favorite photos is of Tony in his den. Although very pale, thin, and ill, he has Cody sitting right beside him, reading him a football magazine.

The book is pretty much a true story. Since I did not have the time or the energy to keep a journal, some events may be slightly enhanced.

The names have been abbreviated for privacy reasons, but believe me, where spoiling Cody is concerned, there are no innocent.

TABLE OF CONTENTS

Foreword 9

Preface 11

The Lull Before The Storm 13

The Great-Grandparents. 17

Hitting the Wall 25

The Search For Hope 51

Cody's Home—Let's Set Our Goals 69

A Cute Little Kid On Crutches. 111

Mainstreaming A Physically Challenged Child—In School
       and In Life 131

The Setback—Accepting the Wheelchair 177

Our Hero 197

The Finish That Goes On. 213

Conclusion. 219

Works Cited 221

FOREWORD

Books are written for many different reasons—some are to educate, others to entertain, and still others to inspire. You are soon to see that this book does all three. As you read Cody's story, you will laugh, cry, learn, and be moved to respond in new ways to your own life's challenges.

Beyond the Steps and Stares could well be subtitled "A Guide to Reaching for the Stars" or "The Primer for Reacting to What Happens in Your Life." Whether you are a student, a teacher, a parent, a healthcare provider, or simply a member of God's great community, you will learn and rejoice as Raina shares with you the story of Cody's struggles and triumphs.

This is the story of remarkable Cody, a true exemplification of the triumph of the human spirit.

~Patrice Delcambre RNC, MSN

PREFACE

IN THE MUD AND SCUM OF THINGS
SOMETHING ALWAYS, ALWAYS SINGS.[1]

It happened on a bleak November afternoon. Standing in the misting rain, facing my mother-in-law's casket, I felt I had finally come to a point where I had to begin to share the story of one special little boy named Cody.

Pain and disappointment have been almost constant companions since his birth, but they have been overshadowed by the blessings of joy and fulfillment that he has brought.

This is Cody's story . . . not complete, because his amazing accomplishments and personality continue to warm all who meet him to this day. Yet as complete as it can be told to this point, for I feel there are so many searching for hope and longing to hear a word of encouragement from others who have faced incredible hardships and survived with faith.

I am his mother and proud to be so. I share his story for many reasons—not only for the families who daily face the challenges of a disability, but also for those who do not. I share in the hope that the able-bodied people who surround Cody and others like him will become more aware of the sensitivity of handicapped individuals, as well as of their attributes and contributions to this world.

This is a story of mixed emotions, from the heartbreak of the lost ideal of a "perfect" child, to the incredibly hilarious events created by this kid. This is a story of happiness and sorrow, accomplishments and failures, and gains and losses, all rolled into the life of one child.

Mainly, I pray that others will find comfort in knowing our family has worked our way through many of the same hardships they may have experienced. I hope some mechanisms for coping may be found through the life of our extraordinary Cody.

CHAPTER 1

The Lull Before The Storm

I'LL DO THE BEST I CAN IN LIFE
THEN SEEK GOD'S HELP
THROUGH STRUGGLE AND STRIFE;
AND WHEN THE TIMES COME
THAT MY PLANS HAVE ALL FAILED
INSTEAD OF CHANGING THE WIND,
I'LL ADJUST THE SAIL.

Raina Futrell

Thirty years of my life had gone by, and I felt I was on top of the world. Paul and I were very much in love and pulled off a story-book wedding in the church I had loved and served for many years, surrounded by our family members and numerous close friends. The reception was fabulous; Mom and Dad loved to open their home to guests for as long as they cared to stay. Mom's brothers and their families from Mississippi and Dad's aunt and cousins from Alabama had come and helped us ready things for several days before the wedding. They were made to stay after the wedding until all the food was gone, which took a while, considering Mom had outdone herself with her culinary skills.

I had expected Mom to cry copious amounts of tears at the wedding, but I did not see even one. I don't know if she was elated that one of us was finally getting married, if she was happy with the fact that she was not required to write any of the 5000 thank you notes, or if the attention of friends and family made her so joyous, but I have never seen her so pleased. I will always derive great pleasure from the memory of her enjoyment of that special time in our lives, which may also be how she survived some of the terrible days that would follow—days we had no inkling were about to unfold.

My dad told me that marriage was 10 percent love and 90 percent toleration, but he had no idea of the strong truth in that. We couldn't see it in the beginning though, and three months after the wedding, when the pregnancy test was positive, we were ecstatic. It seemed like all of our dreams were coming true, and we thanked God every day for our blessings. I didn't even mind the morning sickness, or the noon sickness, or the night sickness, but I was in no way prayed up for the roller coaster ride we were about to go on.

People have always told me, "The Lord won't put any more on you than you can bear." That's true, but in our case He stopped just this side of it and our lives can never be the same. If all of the events of the seventeen years were character-building experiences, then we must be some kind of characters! Still, we were also allowed many joys.

It has always amazed me that so many people, in sharing an opinion of your situation, can penetrate the deepest hurt in your soul, and yet there are those who can share five minutes of encouragement and give you wisdom that you will refer to and rely on the rest of your life. It is mostly the latter group that I will be sharing about in this story.

After the idea of becoming parents had sunk in, Paul or I one would arrive home almost daily with something for the baby. If not from us, then it would be something from my family or his, because everyone was overjoyed at the promise of a new little one. The Christmas season was especially fun. I was almost at the end of my first trimester, and other than the frequent throwing up, everything was wonderful. My doctor was pleased, and the last thing any of us suspected was that there was a problem with the baby.

Throughout the holidays that year, my family seemed closer than they had ever been. The knowledge that there would be a baby born into the family for the first time in many years caused everyone to put aside any old conflicts and draw attention to the coming of our child. Paul's family was no different. His mother had battled a heart defect all of her life. She had been told as a young girl that having children was far too dangerous to her health for it to be possible. After Paul was born, she suffered a terrible episode of congestive heart failure. Nine years later, after his sister's birth, the same thing occurred again. Years later, she realized that she had not only survived to see her children grown and married, but she had witnessed the birth of her daughter's child. Now she would be allowed to share the joy of the birth of her son's child; she felt she had been given a great gift. His dad was also delighted and would often arrive at our house late in the evening after work to visit and make sure I was okay before he went on home. The only grandparents living then were our fathers' mothers and having a new great-grandchild on the way was wonderful news to them both as well.

That first Christmas as a married couple was so perfect. Our families seemed healthy and at peace. We spent a lot of that season gathered around the fireplace, often with friends who dropped by to visit, dreaming of the next Christmas when we would have our own child. I do not know that any of us have known or will ever know again that feeling of freedom from mental burdens. Something in the year of 1986 sent us tumbling down a cliff to encounter a sequence of tragedies that would seem to never end. I know now that moments of peace and contentment in a person's life are treasures and should never be taken lightly. In an instant, the ease and comfort of a peaceful, contented family life can turn to chaos, confusion, and loss, the type of loss that sends you on a pilgrimage for years, searching for a way to salvage home and hope.

CHAPTER 2

The Great-Grandparents . . . Pearl, Aden, Granny Hales, Granny Johns, and Mamaw

*WHEN GROPING FOR ANSWERS
LOST IN THE DARK
THE BEST PLACE TO SEARCH
IS DEEP IN YOUR HEART,
REACHING FOR MEMORIES
FEELING SAD AND ALONE
THE WISDOM OF LOVED ONES
WILL BRING YOU BACK HOME.*

Raina Futrell

It would be impossible to appreciate our family without understanding some of the people who played a big part in our background, particularly our grandparents. Although only one of them ever had a chance to know and love Cody, they gave us some very special gifts that have helped him and us to survive the ordeal we have been forced to live through. The gifts I speak of did not come in pretty boxes or wrapped in paper tied with beautiful bows—for those gifts may bring happiness for the moment—but then they are often put away to catch dust or to be forgotten or even to be misplaced. The gifts I write about here are gifts of their various personalities that have become memories, memories that so often give us an "out" when we come to a point in life that seems hopeless. You really can't look back too much or the past will tear at you until you are only a shell of a person. Yet how very often, over Cody's lifespan, I have reached for one of the memories of those precious people, and suddenly I knew the right answer to what had before seemed like an unsolvable problem.

Not often in Cody's story will I refer to anything of ours as "mine" or "his," because raising Cody takes a maximum effort of all of us, together all the time, but for a moment, in describing our grandparents, I will.

PEARL

Pearl was Mom's mom and the closest person to a saint I have ever known. She loved everyone and was loved by all who knew her. She was born and raised poor and had very little material gain in any part of her life, yet it is she who left me the greatest inheritance anyone could have, her wisdom. She has been gone to Heaven for over twenty years now, and in fact, if she had lived this would have been her 105th year, but I still miss her terribly, as though she just left us.

When I think of Ma, as we lovingly called her and my children call my mother now, I remember how she could cook. People would travel for miles to eat her chicken and dumplings or purple hull peas and cornbread. To this day, I have never seen anyone who could make bigger or better biscuits. I tried to learn, but "cutting the shortening into the flour" just doesn't work well when I do it so we usually eat those canned deals. She taught us to love country cooking. She also taught us about the blessings you could receive in life by keeping your kitchen open to everyone all the time. She showed us how people would drop by to share life's gains and losses in her kitchen, while sharing coffee and teacakes or fried chicken and biscuits with "Norris' Best" syrup. Her kitchen was not fancy, and Lord knows, it wasn't tidy. That dear lady kept every margarine and Cool Whip tub she ever bought on her cabinet, along with a pile of lids, which went into a landslide daily. I don't know if she ever found a lid to fit any of them, but they were there just the same to save leftovers and send food home with people. No one was ever allowed to leave Ma's empty-handed. She sent each and every soul home with teacakes, fig preserves, a watermelon, or something. Some of my best childhood memories are of arriving there on Friday nights after my parents worked until 4:30 P.M. and drove the two hundred miles to get there. We would arrive to find at least twenty-five different dishes cooked. We would eat and visit at the dining table in that kitchen until late into the night.

Ma's was a kitchen full of love; something you don't see much now. People knew when they came there that she would feed them, listen to them, encourage them, and accept them. Therefore, a steady stream of people came in and out of that kitchen. It was cluttered, and there was no air conditioning, but it was a privilege to have been there.

Ma's house burned down some years ago, but my mind often drifts back there. Anytime I smell molasses teacakes, collards, or fried chicken or I see a plastic margarine tub, Cool Whip tub, or flour in twenty-five pound sacks, it takes me back to that kitchen, always full of good home-cooked food and love.

Pearl also taught me about faith. She loved her little country church, and I often think of the weeklong revivals in that church during our summer visits. Those old cardboard fans on a flat stick were all that stood between a heat stroke and us, but we learned about gospel quartet singing and loud preaching. It was during one of those revivals that I dedicated my life to Jesus and began to build a faith that would sustain me in years to come. I also remember my sister and me, standing up behind the cab of our grandparents' old pickup truck, singing hymns as we bounced up and down those old country dirt roads full of ruts. Those are the kind of character-building experiences that you never forget.

Ma witnessed to everyone she could about how the Lord had helped her through all the crises of her life. She was precious to me. The memory of her faith in God lives on for me in so many of her stories, from sending for the preacher when her children had high fevers and how he would sit by the fireplace all night with them and pray along with friends and relatives, to her last days in the hospital, when she called all of us in one by one and made us promise to live on in such a way that we could some day join her in Heaven. These stories spanned a period of over 80 years, and the memory of that kind of faith can sustain you through a lot. She told me once that sometimes people had to reach 100 years old before they realized what was important in life, and I know now that she was right.

Ma also taught me a lot about nature. In my mind, I can still see her in the early morning mist with a bonnet on in a simple dress and apron—both made from flour sacks. She would be wearing some kind of awful shoes, out hoeing that garden and tending those flowerbeds she loved so dearly. Her home was simple, but she had beautiful rose bushes, crepe myrtles, and hydrangeas at each end of the porch. On my spring and summer visits, we would walk over her land. She taught me about the cherry tree blossoms, lily pads on the pond, and even rabbit tobacco. (Yuk!) I see so many people now that don't know collards from pine trees, and I am thankful for the time she spent with me and all that she taught me.

When Ma died, she left me a counted cross-stitch cloth of "The Lord's Prayer." Yet the greatest gift she left me, and my children through me, was a wonderful heritage of knowledge about cooking, how to be nonjudgmental, have faith in every crisis, and how to love and nurture your family and friends and home. Ma loved us unconditionally, and it is that rare trait that I miss her for the most. She also whispered to herself all the time, and Cody does that, so I often refer to him as "little Pearl." That always brings a smile. I will forever treasure the memories of Ma, and I am sure that it was no mistake that she was named Pearl.

ADEN

People often say about couples that opposites attract, and Pearl and Aden were perfect examples of that. Aden, or "Daddy Parker" as many people called him, was a jewel of a person himself, but he and Ma differed in many ways.

Aden was a man of great character and was a real character. In fact, when he and Ma married they were very young and could not obtain permission to marry from his parents. Aden arranged to play the part of a groom and have Ma play the part of a bride in their high school play. He charmed a real preacher from another town to play the part of the preacher assisting with their vows in the play. He arranged a genuine marriage license, and when the play was over, much to the surprise of the entire audience and the preacher, he had Ma's sister announce that they had really married and escaped by way of the horse and buggy she had planted at the back door of the school. What a clown! The whole town, including both sets of parents, had happily watched them marry without objection. Ma said that his mother would pass her walking down the road many times over the next year and turn her head and not speak. She did, however, eventually forgive them both. After all, they had made history by pulling off that little episode.

I have never known anyone who believed in hard work more than Aden did. He would rise around 4 A.M. every day, make a pot of coffee, and drink the entire pot while waiting for the first light of the day. As a child, I often asked him, favoring sleep as I did, why he wanted to get up and wait until it was daylight instead of just sleeping until then. He found that very comical. On our weekend visits, my dad liked to stay up late and watch TV. On one occasion, he was going to bed as Aden was getting up, and as they passed in the hall Aden said, "Son, you and I could run the world. You could take the night shift, and I could take the day shift." His wit was part of his great charisma.

After daylight came, he would put on his overalls and hat and head to the fields. He had gardens all over. When I was growing up, I thought it was normal to drive a pickup truck up and down terraced fields. Those old Chevrolet trucks must have been really well made. He would work without a break until noon, come in for lunch, change overalls because not a dry thread could be found on the first set, eat and rest for fifteen minutes, and then go back and work in the fields until dark. He had this routine until he was 82 years old. I remember Uncle H. telling him once, "Daddy, I am going to hook lights on that mule so you can plow at night."

On Sunday, he went to church. He would be the first in the shower of the only bathroom. Then ten minutes after he went in he would yell, "Pearl, I need a towel." Five minutes later he would yell,"Pearl, I need some underwear." Five minutes after that, "Pearl, where are my clothes?" After he emerged dressed and already sweating because there was no air conditioning, he would request of Pearl his suspenders, hand-kerchief, and hat. Then he would go sit in the truck and blow the horn until the rest of us got ready. Somehow, he had the personality that made you tolerate all of that and still love him dearly.

When he knew we would be visiting for the weekend, he would start pacing the porch at 3 P.M., knowing that Mom and Dad got off work at 4:30 P.M., and then had to face 200 miles of Friday traffic. He would be worn out when we got there, but never failed to show us a good time. He had a real art for telling stories. When we would leave on Sunday afternoons, we always left him crying. To this day, I can hardly stand to say good-bye to guests on Sunday afternoon.

Aden did his part of teaching us about nature, mostly about gardening. From him I learned about pushing a plow and giving life all you have to give. He took great pride in his gardens and grew vegetables for all of his children and grandchildren as long as he lived. Growing up, I thought the only vacation that working people had was going to their parents' farm and canning vegetables. I miss those times now—visiting with my cousins and sitting in the back of Aden's pickup shucking corn while the babies slept in front of a box fan on a pallet made with quilts.

Aden also introduced me to fishing. He would have us rise at daylight, pack a lunch of Vienna sausage, sardines (Yuk!), watermelon, crackers, and cheese, and drive down to his pond. We caught a lot of fence, bushes, and a few fish, but mostly we learned how to have a lazy, fun, summer day to remember forever.

Whenever I see an older man in overalls, wearing a hat, pouring coffee in a saucer to blow on it before drinking it, telling a dynamic old tale, and smelling of Old Spice After Shave Lotion, I miss Aden. His wit and gift of gab, passed on, have helped my family, Cody, and me to know how to lighten up and laugh when things are too intense to survive any other way.

Sometimes my thoughts slide back to cool summer evenings, sitting out under the chinaberry trees in that old metal glider, listening to Aden tell stories and line everyone up for the next day, and I really wish he were still around. I will also never forget, at the age of 13, walking the aisle of that country church and kneeling to accept Christ and then feeling Aden's arm around my shoulder.

My grandparents were jewels. I think of them anytime I see an aluminum water dipper or hear a screen door slam shut. Back when they were such an important part of my life, I had no idea how often and how deeply my family and I would draw from all of the wonderful things that they were.

GRANNY JOHNS

She was Paul's grandmother, and he was very close to her. She died before we were married, but I knew her a little when we were dating. I do know she took Paul on a lot of special outings when he was growing up. She was the type of lady who could be seen in town eating lunch with her grandchildren, one at a time. Her husband died when Paul's mom was 10, and she raised her alone at a time when that was very difficult to do. She was sweet and comical, and he speaks often of their trips together and how much she loved him.

GRANNY HALES

She was my dad's mom, and she had the will of an iron horse. Her husband died in his 50s, and with Dad already married to Mom, it left her totally alone with no skills or work background. She went to New Orleans all by herself, rented an apartment in the French Quarter, and took a course on supervising a housekeeping department of a hospital. She was 60 years old when she did that. On low energy days, I think of a sixty-year-old widow driving herself to that huge city, pulling a U-Haul behind her car, searching out a place to live, and training for her first career, and my pity party ends. Both of our "grannies" taught us how to be persistent and independent.

MAMAW

She was Paul's paternal grandmother and the only one of our grandparents who knew Cody. At 83 years old, she lived alone in her own home, still drove like a racecar driver, packed a .38 caliber, long-barreled pistol, and backed up from no one. She and Cody were big buddies, and even though he alluded way too often to how "old" she was, he loved for her to come and stay with us. She and Cody created some hilarious events together.

CHAPTER 3

Hitting the Wall

WE MUST NOT HOPE TO BE MOWERS,
AND TO GATHER THE RIPE GOLD EARS,
UNLESS WE HAVE FIRST BEEN SOWERS
AND WATERED THE FURROWS WITH TEARS.
IT IS NOT JUST AS WE TAKE IT,
THIS MYSTICAL WORLD OF OURS,
LIFE'S FIELD WILL YIELD AS WE MAKE IT
A HARVEST OF THORNS OR OF FLOWERS.[2]

Perseverance by
Johann Wolfgang von Goethe (1749–1832)

When asked before a baby is born if they want a boy or a girl, many parents will reply, "I don't care as long as it's healthy." I'm not sure if Paul and I said that or not, but our baby being born healthy was not our destiny. Psychologists say that 85 percent of what you worry about never happens. For us, the 15 percent that did happen surely was life altering.

The two ultrasounds done at the doctor's office during my pregnancy had been very exciting. We could tell the baby was a boy, and we could see the heart beating. Due to the lack of quality of ultrasounds in the area where we lived at the time, most people, including us, just pretended to see something more. The people who did the ultrasounds would be so confident about what they saw that we were not about to admit that he looked like an alien swimming in grape jelly to us. Of course, before the event is over they give you a picture, which you proudly display in your family room. You thrust that picture in the face of every visitor, especially family members, who are quick to say things like, "His head is shaped just like mine."

You want to reply, "The lady doing the scan said that was his shoulder," but you just cannot do it. So you all pretend together that you know what in the heck you are looking at. As it turns out, one of the most awful things a person can possess is a false sense of security. Somehow, that makes the shattering of a dream so much more difficult to understand and tolerate.

Looking back now, I realize that even though our dream was about to be forever altered, it is an amazing thing when fate takes a hand. The unbelievable Divine intervention that took place afforded Cody a better life than he would otherwise have been able to have.

In the first part of July of 1986, Paul and I were getting very excited as we awaited a due date of August 16, the day before our first anniversary. I was large, I tired easily, and what little I slept was in a recliner. Having been a stomach sleeper prior to pregnancy, sleep did not come easily. Since turning on my stomach at that point lifted me three feet in the air, I just spent nights in the recliner, pretending I slept well. Dreaming of the baby was sweet though, even if I was awake.

Supervising a neonatal intensive care unit and a newborn nursery happens to be my profession, and when I arrived at work that July morning things seemed to be "business as usual," with one exception. That exception would give me the push off the cliff that I still continue to tumble down at times, but no one there had any idea what was about to happen.

It is often true that the most dramatic days of our lives give us no warning. Everything seems so normal and calm, and at the end of that day, you know in your heart and mind that you are changed forever. It happens when loved ones are killed and you get one of those terrible phone calls that you never want to receive. It happens when children are abducted. It happens when a home burns to the ground, and for us, it all started with an ultrasound.

Summer is a very busy season in the NICU, and that day was true to form. When you supervise 30 women, deliver 250 babies a month, and do transports in and out, there is always a lot of confusion. This is so true that quiet summer days make you nervous.

Three hours into that busy day, I got a call that a sales person from California was in the hospital and wanted to show us a brand new ultrasound machine, superior to any previously on the market. I was busy, I was irritated, and I was eight months pregnant. Yet fortunately, because we are always aiming for the best patient outcomes possible and because she had traveled all the way from California, I felt obligated to allow the lady to show us the machine.

As is true, most life-altering days start out without suspicion. In addition, there are often people you are associated with every day for years and you have no clue that one day they will perform an act that will rescue you from something awful. One of the doctors I worked with was that person for me, and I will be indebted to him for all of my life.

Now allowing an ultrasound to be done in front of my entire staff was not an idea I was crazy about, but I had a lot of encouragement. Since I was eight months pregnant, a lot could be seen, and I had already been told the baby was fine. So after a promise that the lights would be out and that I would be properly draped before my big belly was exposed and covered with gel, I agreed.

During the show, a room full of nurses and doctors sat in complete amazement at the high quality of the machine and made comments about how cute he looked and all the different organs that could be plainly seen. We were favorably impressed, to say the least, and everyone in the room was delighted except the operator and one other person, Dr. A. As a traveling sales person, I am sure the lady was taught not to get involved in people's pregnancies, but rather to demonstrate the machine, leave a contact number, and move on. I am not sure if that lady had even a clue of the impact that tape would make in our lives. All I remember of her is that she gave me a picture that was made while he was facing forward, information on how the machine could be ordered, her thanks for allowing her to do her demonstration on a busy day, and her walking out of my life. I could have imagined it, but I faintly remember seeing something disturbing in her eyes when we shook hands good-bye. I just passed it off as her having a plane to catch and a busy schedule to follow. Thinking back, perhaps she was an angel among us who quietly did her job and faded away.

Right after we completed the ultrasound, I heard Dr. A. saying to the operator several times as I cleaned jelly off my belly, "Isn't that different?" She was hesitant and finally gave him the film to keep and review. However, Dr.A., was an intelligent and inquisitive man, and the staff and I just thought he wanted to use the tape to further develop his knowledge of ultrasounds. The possibility of a problem with the baby never crossed my mind. He took the tape and left, and the rest of us went back to work. It turned out to be a busy but pleasant day, and I was anxious to get home and show Paul the new picture. I actually felt reassured that everything with the baby was fine.

Late that afternoon as my shift was near the end, I saw Dr. A. out in the parking lot of the hospital. I saw him go out to his car and come back in a couple of times and I remember thinking, *He must be really tired to be that forgetful.* A moment later someone told me he wanted to see me in the back hall by the transport incubators. I thought, *Uh oh,* because that is where I was normally summoned when a mistake had been made by the staff. There I would be given instructions on how to handle the incident without the entire staff hearing our conversation. As a head nurse, I was used to "putting out fires," so I went bouncing back there, but an unfamiliar look in his eyes caused me to stop dead in my tracks. Innocently I asked, "What is it Dr. A.?" Later on, in an irrational moment I thought, *I should have never asked or even gone back there,* as if that would have changed anything.

Dr. A. spoke quietly and sadly, "I have something to tell you that I would rather not."

Still never imagining he had something personal to tell me, I said, "Oh, what could be that bad? You have been keeping me straight for eight years now. I am sure together we can make a workable plan." At that point, I saw moisture in his eyes and my heart sank. My next question sounded like the words were an echo in a tunnel, "What's wrong?"

The next few minutes are ones I will forever wish I could erase from my life. The words that rolled out changed everything, and it seemed like they hung suspended in the air forever. Many times I have wanted to rub them out, run away from them, or do anything to make them not true, but unfortunately, life just doesn't work that way.

He began with, "Three times I have tried to leave and not tell you, but we have worked together and been friends for too long, and I knew you would feel like I betrayed you. Either way I go, I have already overstepped my boundaries." Then came the most terrible words I had ever heard, "We think the baby has spina bifida."

Hoping that denial would mean he was not talking about my baby I said, "What baby?"

He swallowed hard and made it a reality with one word, "Yours." My knees weakened, and apparently, all the color left my face because Dr. A. quickly pushed a chair under me, and I collapsed into it. He was frightened and began to speak very fast, "I took the ultrasound tape to the radiologist this morning because the spine looked unusual to me, and he said there was definitely a problem. We called your OB doctor and sent the tape to him for viewing. He is going to compare it to the ones done in his office earlier and call you. You know no place in this area has that machine, and it could be a mistake. Don't tell Paul until you hear from your OB doctor. I have to go, and I will check on you later. I am so sorry. Call me if you need me for anything." Then he was gone and I was left in total shock.

I went back in the NICU in a fog and the other RN working with me said, "My God, what's wrong?" I must have looked awful. Between sobs I began to try to tell her and she kept saying, "Oh, no!" I felt sick and scared and faint. Needless to say, she sent me home.

I'm really not sure how I drove those ten miles in heavy traffic on the interstate to my house that afternoon, but I did. When I got there, nobody was home and I was glad. Still in total disbelief, I collapsed into the recliner and began to try to remember what I had learned in nursing school about spina bifida. All I could remember was that the spine is open at birth, paralysis is present, and the babies often need shunts to drain excessive fluid off the brain. Nothing good. Many images rushed through my mind, and I felt more ill and scared and alone than I had ever felt in my life. My chest felt heavy, my abdomen was heavy, and a large lump formed in my throat, a lump that is still there all these years later. Making the conversion from the happiest time in your life to the saddest in a one-hour period is unbelievably hard.

My mom always taught us that whatever the crisis was that we should sit down, eat a good meal, and everything would be okay. (One of my best friends and I joke that she was always told to go and put on fresh lipstick. That's why my sister and I are overweight, and she and her sister are thin and Mary Kay representatives.) That would not work at all, so I decided to take a hot bath. I cried so much in there just sitting and staring at my belly and talking to my unborn child that I was near passing out. As the time neared for Paul to get home from work I decided that since his father was newly diagnosed with terminal cancer, his mother was in and out of congestive heart failure, and my dad had moved in with a strange woman after 33 years of solid married life, I needed to break this to him gently. So I regained my composure as best I could and waited for his arrival.

As fate would have it, he arrived home on time in a really good mood, and the first thing he said was, "Let's go out and eat." I almost fainted. In the back of my mind, though, I kept thinking of Dr. A. saying, "Don't tell Paul until you hear from your OB doctor."

He said, "I'm just going to wash up, and I'll wait and take a bath when we get back so we can beat the dinner crowd." The only comment he made was,"You look really tired, you must have had a hard day."

"You have no idea."

He responded, "Well, I'm tired too. As soon as we get back and I can take a bath, we'll go to bed early because neither one of us has really slept well or undisturbed for several weeks worrying about all of our parents' crises, and soon we will have a little bundle to keep us awake anyway."

I whispered, "Okay." However, in my mind I was thinking, *We might never sleep well again the rest of our lives.* My head was reeling as I got in the car. *How in the world can I tell him . . . ? There is no way any of our parents can handle this new burden . . . God help me to survive this day and the next month. . . . How can I make it through dinner without passing out?* I knew I had to try. I can hardly remember the drive to the cafeteria, just Paul talking about work and his dad's chemotherapy and the baby. I was trying to answer what broken parts of questions I could focus on.

As we pulled into the parking lot he asked, "You are not having labor pains are you?"

My comeback was, "No. I just have a lot on my mind."

He said, "Well, I'll tell you like Ma would, 'Let's eat a good meal and you'll feel a lot better.' " He laughed. My thoughts were, *I hope that isn't your last time to laugh for a great while because you deserve to be able to enjoy this baby, and I hope someone here knows how to do the Heimlich maneuver on a pregnant lady because when I try to eat I'll probably need it done to unchoke me.*

We went through the line, and I got a bowl of soup, a roll, and a glass of tea. He got a full meal and commented, "Baby, I am so glad I brought you out to eat that."

I answered wearily, "Oh, I am just not very hungry." We sat down at the table, I took one bite of roll, and this wave of horror rolled over me. I have never been very good at deceit, and I wanted to share this grief with my partner in life, my love, the father of the baby. I ran to the restroom and was ill. I made a scene in there and some lady kept trying to help me. I just wanted to get out of there as fast as I could.

When I finally regained composure well enough to return to the table, Paul was sitting there with a petrified look on his face, his food pushed away from him, and he demanded, "Whatever it is, you might as well tell me. You know we are too close for you to lie, and I don't think there could be anything worse than what we are already living through with our parents. After all, I know I will have to give up both of mine soon."

I thought, *Well, we are about to find out.* He was in denial, and I wanted so much to leave him in denial, but I knew that I couldn't. So I said, "Okay, I'll tell you, but not here."

We left our food on the table, untouched, paid, and went to the car. I broke down. Paul was speechless. The moment was horrible. After I gained a little control he declared, "I'm not moving until you tell me. You need to tell me and I need to know."

So, as gently as I could I related the events of the day. He said nothing. He started the car and drove home. All the way there, I cried and he said not one word. I pleaded, "Paul, please say something." I knew he couldn't. Arriving home, he went straight to the bathroom and started running his bath water. I stopped in the den and sat down. I thought, *Okay, he needs a moment to himself. I'll give him that.*

After about ten minutes I could not stand it any longer, I went into the bathroom. He was sitting in that huge tub with tears streaming down his cheeks and his tortured words were, "This is hard to take. This is really hard to take." I felt sick.

A moment later the phone rang. It was my OB doctor. He instructed, "Raina, Paul and you and I need to talk. I want you to come to my office at 10 A.M. Monday morning. Remember, 15 percent of the time these ultrasounds are wrong. Try not to worry too much. Monday morning we will go over all the options and make our plan. Try to rest over the weekend, and I will see you then. Write down all of your questions."

I can't remember saying anything. I do remember thinking, *Why does everything bad happen late Friday afternoon so you have to suffer through a weekend? I'm sure not putting my faith in the 15 percent of wrong ultrasounds. God help me to face this "plan" he is talking about.*

Paul was so upset. He asked me, "How in the world are we going to tell our families?"

I really didn't know the answer to that. He then said, "I need to drive around and be by myself for a while." I told him that was okay, but it wasn't okay. Nothing was okay now, and I wondered if it ever would be again. I told him to be careful and he left. I turned the ringer off on the phone and collapsed on the bed, crying uncontrollably. I couldn't talk or pray. I was so afraid I would go into labor.

After three hours Paul returned, and he looked amazingly in control and did not smell of liquor. (He did not drink but you never know what that type of stress will do to someone.) He had one long-stemmed rose for me. He spoke with a quiet, calm voice, "God will help us to get through this. He is still our baby no matter what, and we have each other."

I was so touched and knew I should say something profound, but all I could do was hug him and whisper, "Okay."

So we were forced into a weekend of waiting, waiting which would become typical of our lives over the next few years. No symptoms, no events, no information, just waiting under the cloud of an awful dread. Sometimes you don't even have enough information to know what it is that you dread.

We had decided not to tell our families until we knew more or until we had to, but very often God has a plan that is different from ours. On Saturday morning Paul's mother and sister and my mother arrived at our house at the same time (which almost never happened), and I knew it was time to tell them. We needed them to talk to; we had cried and stared at the walls all night. Both of us looked terrible, and as Colin

Powell says, "Bad news does not get better with age."[3] What exactly we said to them is a blur but the response of all three was the same, "That just cannot be true. We don't believe it." Even though my nursing training had taught me that the first stage of grief is denial, I was bewildered. Paul and I were actually at a loss of what to do next. All three of them told us not to worry or cry because it was all just some kind of bad mistake. I told them all, "As much as I wish you were all right, I know it is true. The radiologist was very sure." A few minutes later they left, still in total denial. Another truth to life is that the support you seek so desperately is not always there because predicting people's reactions to a crisis is not always possible. It had never occurred to us that they would react with total denial.

The word spread like wildfire after that. Bad news always does, and your dearest friends and family call to pledge their loyalty, but then there are also the curiosity seekers. The calls became too much by Sunday afternoon, and I turned the phone off. I hated to do that, but the stress of saying it over and over again was too much. Paul decided he would go for a drive, but I didn't want to go. He left and I began to spiral down into a deep depression.

By Monday morning, the news had really taken its toll on both of us. We dressed and drove to the doctor's office in silence. I had no list of questions, because I felt like he was going to tell me more than I wanted to know anyway. He already had. The mood was grim and so different from all the other visits there when I had been so happy and excited. As we entered his fine office and sat in the big, pretty wingback chairs, I felt sick. *Why do we have to be here? Why can't things be okay?* It was one of many moments when you truly know you cannot find a pot of gold at the end of the rainbow, and life is no work of art.

The doctor was very kind and he tried to accentuate the positives, but I only felt waves of fear and horror. Paul, on the other hand, began to fire a very organized list of informed questions at him. I was amazed and astonished. He had never heard of spina bifida three days before. The doctor was only partially able to satisfy him with answers.

He told us to cancel the 48-hour stay plans at our selected hospital and arrange to go to another area hospital where the Level III NICU and neonatologists and the neurosurgeon were available. He gave us a

Monday morning C-section date three weeks away, and he tried to reassure us he would help us through all of it. The reality of it only became more intense and scary for me.

As we started down the hall to go out, we met his nurse. She embraced us and cried with us. She also assured us that she would be there during the C-section and close by during the first few days in the hospital. She told us we could call her anytime. I knew she was true to her word, and she was such a fabulous nurse and person that Paul and I both felt better. God sends angels when you need them, and, Praise the Lord, that would not be the only time he sent her.

In the car, I turned to Paul and inquired, "If you have never heard of spina bifida, how could you know all of those questions to ask?"

He came back with, "I knew you would tell me only what you wanted me to know and the least hurtful things, so I went to the library at the university and looked up all the information I could find about it and made my list of questions for the doctor. See, you can't boss me around like you thought you could, can you?"

My reaction was, "No, and I wouldn't have married you if I had known that." It would be one of the few times a conversation about spina bifida would have any humor in it.

The next two weeks were the worst of my life to date. I went to work as scheduled and so did Paul. I knew sitting alone in our house, falling deeper into depression, would not help the baby or me either one. I am sure I was almost useless at work, and looking at the sick babies in the NICU was almost unbearable. However, my friends there who were doctors and nurses and other medical people helped me to brace myself because they knew about spina bifida. They even knew some positive things and how other people had learned to cope with handicapped children. It was so odd, because I had been referring people to Handicapped Children's Services for years. I can't really say I had no compassion for those families because I have tried to live by Christian principles since I became a Christian at thirteen. Yet after facing a birth defect in my own child and all of the sequence of events that followed, I have certainly seen things from a different perspective. As a matter of fact, I believe the families who have had babies in the NICU since Cody's birth have all received more empathy from me, at least I hope so. The saying, "Walk a mile in my shoes" is true.

Every day that drew nearer to delivery became more difficult. I cried so much and kept down so little food and liquids that I became dehydrated. The doctor wanted to put me in the hospital and give me IV fluids, but I begged out of that. I felt like that would finish me off before I even delivered.

The doctor set the C-section for a Monday morning when I would be 37 weeks pregnant. The next to the last visit to his office, two weeks before the section date, was awful. I had lost 27 pounds during my pregnancy, my blood pressure was high, I was dehydrated, and I was physically and emotionally drained. Once again, the wonderful nurse who had become an angel in our lives assured me she would be right with us. She told me she would come at 6 A.M. on Monday morning since the C-section was set for 8 A.M., and she promised we would all get through it together. Because she was one who lights up the whole room just by walking in, we took great comfort in her promise. She was beautiful and kind and someone who had been to "handle it" school, so I knew she could help us manage whatever happened in the delivery room. We considered it a privilege to have her with us as well as just to have her in our lives.

My spirits weakened with every passing day. It was hard to believe I could cry that much and still keep going. The last week before the delivery, the Director of Nurses, who was my friend and mentor, came to me and insisted that I take off. Even though I knew I was not in any shape physically and emotionally to keep working (especially with sick babies and their families), I argued because I wanted to have as much time as possible to spend with the baby after he was born. My boss was right though; I was at a point where I would sit and stare and the tears would flow. I didn't even know where the tears came from anymore. I had no business trying to work and manage a critical care unit.

The following Tuesday was my last doctor's visit before being admitted to the hospital. When we went to the doctor's office that morning his nurse was waiting to talk to us. She told us that she was going out of town the next day until that Sunday, but reassured us she would be there very early on Monday morning, before I went to surgery. She promised to pray for us over the weekend. We cried and hugged, and then we were given orders to go the next afternoon to the hospital and have an ultrasound done. Many times over the last seventeen years, the fact has been reinforced in our lives that, except for God's love, nothing is for sure.

The ultrasound process began at 1 P.M. and was not completed until 3 P.M. As I lay flat on that table and witnessed the measuring of the defect and of his head at many different angles, my sadness turned to sheer panic. The ultrasound technician tried to make comforting conversation, but I said nothing. I was completely choked. I know her job would have been easier if I could have answered some of her questions and concerns, but God alone knows what a terrible experience the whole procedure was. When I stood up at the end, the whole room was spinning; I made it to the rest room and fainted. I was only out for a minute and I begged Paul, "Please, just get me home." The technician wanted to call my doctor, but I assured her he had checked me the day before, and I was okay. I knew it was the panic imposed by viewing the ultrasound coupled with lying flat for too long that caused the fainting. I promised to go straight home to bed, that Paul would not leave me, and that I would call the doctor if I needed further attention. Reluctantly, she let me go.

As we drove home, we were both speechless. Not even in our wildest dreams would we have expected to have these feelings right before the baby was born. I suppose all expectant parents have waves of unrest, but this was sheer panic and horror, moments you never really get over. We both knew we had to do something, so we planned to go to church at 6 P.M., two hours later, with the hope of finding comfort in God's house among people who loved us. Dressing for church was so difficult. Besides being huge, I was wiped out, but I have never felt more led to go.

Well, as fate would have it, my mother asked if she could go with us that night. I know it was because we were so upset and frightened, since she had never been to that church before. On the way there, she and Paul kept asking me, "What happened during the ultrasound today that caused you to be so upset?"

I kept saying, "I don't know, just the whole thing." I wasn't about to tell them that part of the time his head looked the size of Frankenstein's. I couldn't make any sense of it, and I wasn't about to have the two people I loved most in the world suffering as much as I was, if I could block that. Even as I sit and write this now, I can tell you that was the beginning of a truth I often verbalize, "Paul comes close, but God alone knows what I have been through." Some things just don't need to be said if telling them will only cause more suffering. So I never told them.

Upon arrival at church, everyone there was surprised but delighted to see us. We only wanted to make it to the end of the service so we could go down to the altar and ask all of them to pray for us, knowing they would willingly do so, but it never happened. Ten minutes into the service, during the singing, I began to feel different. It wasn't pain; in fact, it is hard to describe, but the rhythm of it got my attention. I leaned over to Paul and told him to give me his watch. His eyes became huge and his question was, "Why?"

Not wanting to disrupt church and because Paul cannot whisper, I said, "Please, just give it to me." When he did, I timed these "quivers" in my belly and discovered they were exactly three minutes apart. I was astounded.

I kept hearing my OB doctor say, "Whatever you do, get to the hospital as soon as labor starts, if it does, because if we don't do the C-section, the spinal cord will be more damaged and the baby will have more severe problems."

I didn't want Paul and Mom to panic, and I sure didn't want the whole congregation to panic and follow us to the hospital or anything crazy like that. I leaned over to Paul's ear and stated as calmly as I could, "We have to go."

He responded immediately in his non-whispering tone, "Why? What's wrong?"

I condensed my reply to, "I don't feel well." I thought he would believe that and exit without a scene, but he knows me too well.

He could tell by my face that something else was going on. He snapped back, with a tone that sounded to me like it was on a loud speaker, "Tell me the truth!"

I begged him, "Paul, please. Let's go and I will explain." I was so scared and I am not sure how much of a scene we made leaving, but it must not have been too bad, since none of the church people followed us.

Once outside the church, I told Paul and Mom I believed I was in labor, and the contractions were growing closer together. I explained to them the importance of immediately getting to the hospital in time to do a C-section. Well, that was more information than ol' Paul could be safe with. As soon as we were all three in the car and the last door shut, he disrupted half of the gravel in the church drive. For the rest of the ten miles back to our house, I thought I was on a roller coaster ride at Disney World. The road was two lanes and he put the pedal to the metal, passed log trucks over double yellow lines, ran red lights, and almost ran over the top of cars in front of us. All Paul needed that night was a siren and a red flashing light and he could have posed as any rescue vehicle in the parish. That is exactly what someone needs who is trying *not* to deliver a baby. When we arrived at our house, the contractions were coming two minutes apart. I asked my mother to go in the bedroom and get my suitcase (already packed, thank God), and I called the OB answering service.

As far as I can remember, that night was my first encounter of frustration trying to find a doctor during a crisis. It would in no way be my last. On the first call, the answering service assured me they would find him quickly after I explained the situation. I believed them. Twenty minutes later the contractions were more intense, and I could feel my blood pressure rising. I called again. This time the answering service worker sounded unconcerned as she said, "Oh yeah, I was going to try to call him at home, wasn't I?" I had no patience for her apathy when my not getting to the hospital in time to do the section could alter my baby's life in a negative way. I couldn't understand the lack of training or at least the lack of concerned response from her. (I was young. If that happened today, I would not be surprised.) I knew I had to take charge.

Paul kept asking, "Are you hurting?"

I kept telling him, "No, but the contractions are exactly two minutes apart." He kept insisting that he had never heard of labor without pain. I insisted we get in the car and go to the hospital.

Sarcastically, he asked, "Do you want me to take the suitcase?"

With a grimace I answered, "Either that or you can come back later and get it."

His disbelieving tone would soon change. On the way to the hospital, he turned to me and said, "Now, let me get this straight. We are going to just show up on the labor unit like the Beverly Hillbillies and announce we need our doctor?"

I stated dryly, "As soon as possible."

He replied, "Okay." That was our total conversation in the car. The rest of the way I silently begged God for help. The whole thing was one big adventure. It still is.

Our first encounter upon our arrival at the hospital was the security guard planted just inside the door. By now, it was 9:45 P.M. When we left the church, it had been 7:15 P.M. It was only ten minutes from our house to the hospital. I kept thinking, *Why does everything have to be a challenge? I am exhausted and the baby hasn't even been born yet.* The security guard wanted us to sign in until Paul exclaimed, "Man, can't you see she is having a baby?" Then he wanted us to hurry past his post. By the time we were on the elevator, all three of us had worked our way into sweaty, hypertensive states and nobody talked. We arrived at the Labor Unit nurses' station, and I could not help but feel that we were the picture of what Paul had predicted . . ."the Beverly Hillbillies."

As I will say many times during this story, God puts angels in your path when you need them. As you can imagine, walking into a labor unit unannounced, in labor, with no doctor in tow, is neither normal nor desirable for the staff, the mother, or the family. I was fearful we would not be received well, but as often happens, I underestimated God's plan.

Just as the nurse was about to explain the proper admitting procedures for that hospital, Lucille appeared. She was best friend to Robbie, our long-term friend and housekeeper. Robbie stayed with my sister and me from the time I was two weeks old until I started to school, and she was very dear to my heart. Mom and I knew Lucille very well. Paul had never heard of her, but at that point, he was searching for any port in the storm. Before the charge nurse could finish her unwanted instructions, Lucille appeared at the desk. She knew our situation so she immediately blurted out, "Raina, what in the world are you doing here this time of night?"

That was a question I was desperate to answer. All I really had to say to her, a nursing assistant and mother of another nurse manager at my hospital, was, "I am about to have this baby." She kicked it into gear after that.

The charge nurse seemed irritated because we had arrived near the end of her shift, but Lucille quickly convinced her that checking me was of the utmost importance. To deliver a baby, a woman must usually dilate nine to ten centimeters, I was already dilated to a five, and I was laboring fast. All of a sudden, the whole staff went into action. It seemed like within a few minutes I had signed a trainload of papers, and Dr. H., my OB doctor, appeared. He explained that he had gone to dinner with his wife to celebrate an anniversary for the first time in years and the doctor on call was already in an emergency section so he couldn't answer his page. The nurses put in an IV and urinary catheter and dressed me in one of those "beautiful" hospital gowns. Next they quickly moved me to a stretcher (with some degree of difficulty, needless to say). When I looked up, Mom and Paul were on either side of me, crying. I said, "This is it. We are going to have this baby."

Mom's promise was, "I'll be praying."

And Paul's parting words were, "I love you, and I will come back there as soon as they will let me." That was all that was said. It just didn't seem like enough. Words can't really buffer moments like that. Words are never enough.

As they rolled me down the hall, Dr. H. was running alongside, pulling on shoe covers, making some comment about how I had not done anything like he told me to since I got pregnant, and trying to help me not to be so nervous. Then suddenly a man appeared beside the stretcher introducing himself as Dr. J., the neurosurgeon. He immediately started complaining about not being able to come to my hospital room on Sunday night before the scheduled section on Monday morning and explain all the details of spina bifida and the required neurosurgery. He told me he did not like my signing consents in the hall without being fully informed. He sounded mad, and he sounded like he thought I had planned it that way. Next the nurse manager of OB appeared and asked what she could do to help me. I am sure they had called her in to help during my delivery. I whispered, "Please, reroute that little neurosurgeon so he can't run down the hall by this stretcher fussing at me." She laughed.

As we burst through the doors of the C-section surgical room, fear gripped me so I prayed. Now that little cold table they move you onto feels like it is only six inches wide. I am sure it is much wider, but it didn't feel like it, and it was so cold. The first thing that happened in there was the appearance of the anesthesiologist, a doctor I had seen and met during my nursing clinicals, ten years before. He asked me to roll on my side and put my knees up to my chin. Is that ridiculous or what? I remember pointing to my abdomen and asking, "Okay, but where is he supposed to go?" He found that amusing. He quickly performed the spinal without difficulty. I was so thankful for his skill, but before that event was over, he had helped me even more in a very special way.

During the course of the surgery, he asked me if I knew the neurosurgeon. He chuckled when I relayed our moments of introduction from my stretcher, and then he told me this story. He said, "When Dr. J. first moved here a few years back, I was called out one night to do anesthesia on a mother and a newborn with spina bifida. I came prepared to be there for several hours as was required by previous neurosurgeons I worked with—what I call "spending the night." I readied my supplies and he did too—to repair the open spine on the baby. He walked over to me before he started, with his hands in sterile gloves folded together and asked, 'What can I do to help you?' I just shook my head in a negative direction because I wasn't sure what he was asking me, since neurosurgeons don't usually assist anesthesia staff. He replied, 'Good. We will be finished in thirty minutes.' I found that comical because of the number of all-night surgeries I had witnessed. Guess what? Twenty-nine minutes after he started, he was popping his gloves into the garbage. Finished. A beautiful surgery done by the most skilled hands I had ever seen." Very shortly, I would take great comfort in that story. Dr. R. was another one of God's angels put in my path to help me.

After the spinal, I was placed flat on my back and a drape was mounted in front of me, a drape on a bar shaped like an upside down U, so I could not see what the OB doctors were doing. I was glad; I didn't want to see. I did not want to be there. I wanted to scream and shake the rafters with, "God, why does it have to be this way?" but I didn't. I just kept praying—one last plea for spina bifida not to become part of our lives. Sometimes God answers our prayers with a "No." That was one of them.

Just prior to the beginning of the surgery, another doctor came in with gown, gloves, and mask on, and I wondered if Dr. H. was expecting to have trouble getting the baby out or if it was the neonatologist.

As it turned out, it was the doctor on call. He had finished with the previous section then heard I was there and decided to come and help Dr. H. When he got to the side of the table, I realized I knew him. He only had been in practice for a couple of years and just prior to opening his practice had completed his residency at the hospital where I worked and managed the NICU. That area was not his favorite; OB was, so I had helped him to get through it. We had become friends. Now here he was, just when I was thinking, *I wish Dr. H.'s nurse could be here. I sure could use a friend right about now.*

Over the next seventeen years, whenever I needed God, He would show up in a doctor, nurse, therapist, nurse assistant, preacher, coach . . . someone. That doctor was the perfect friend in the absence of Dr. H.'s nurse, who would later appear to rescue me many times in this story, but who was out of town that night. This doctor was kind, funny, and sensitive. He knew neither Paul nor Mom would be allowed in there, but he would. Moreover, I would need a friend, so he came. He never even sent me a bill. (I loved that!) A few months later I learned that he had become an expert at interpreting OB ultrasounds, and the new machine the California sales lady had shown the day we discovered my baby had spina bifida had been purchased for our area. I was told that comparing the quality of the tapes from the old and new machines (both used to do my ultrasounds) had been a big influence in convincing the area doctors that the big price tag was worth it when it helped babies like mine to have a better outcome. I was glad. Good always comes out of bad.

Now came the big question from the OB doctor, "Are you ready?" How dumb is that? If he had to wait until I was ready, we would still be there now—seventeen years later. In addition, what could I do to get ready, lying flat with IV's and a catheter and drapes holding me down?

Still, as if it were a requirement to give the expected response, I replied, "Cut away." He did just that. With the knife, he cut away what was left of my identity up to then. He ended an era, a journey up to the point of becoming a mother, taking on a new identity, and a plunge into the unknown. Excited, scared, unprepared in many ways, and there was no book of instructions—just faith, family, friends, and our health-care team. It would be enough, but at times like that one, it wouldn't seem to be.

As they made the cut, Dr. R. started to put an oxygen mask over my face, and I rebelled emphatically, "I don't need that!"

He laughed and said, "It's for the baby!"

"Well, okay. Put it on then," was my reply. That was stupid on my part; I knew that. The intensity of that event had my mind clouded. Then to make matters worse, even though the spinal had rendered my paralyzed, as it is designed to do, I was convinced that my legs were falling off to the right of the table. I kept telling them that.

At first, my doctor friend was polite and replied each time, "I can see your legs, and they are on the table."

However, after several episodes of my making remarks like, "Y'all are going to be sorry. The baby is going to fall out on the floor."

They looked at each other and then at me and said simultaneously, "Please shut up." That was the last time I mentioned my legs.

Next came nausea. I remarked to Dr. H., "I am so nauseated."

I know he was attempting to keep me upbeat when he leaned around the drapes for a moment and said, "What's new about that?" He was right. Nausea had been my companion for nine months. Why should that night be any different? Suddenly the baby was out, and it seemed like an eternity before he cried as both doctors shouted, "It's a boy!" I knew that. I wanted to know if he had spina bifida, if he was breathing okay, how bad it was, something of comfort. Soon I was to receive more information than I could disseminate the rest of my life.

The moment it was possible, the nurse brought him for me to see. He had a beautiful face and his hair looked red. I liked that. The rest of him from the neck down was wrapped in sterile sheets, and I thought, *Oh, my God, his body is so mangled they won't even show it to me.* Another idiotic moment. Of course, they were just keeping the opening in the spine in a sterile environment. I had been taught that in nursing school, and throughout the years, I had taught many nurses to do that. When you are frightened and overwhelmed, all knowledge and reason flee.

Still, I was not going to miss that opportunity to introduce myself to and bond with my son, because I was not sure if I would have another chance. So I put my face next to his and I said, in the sweetest tone I could, "Hi, Buddy! I'm your mom and you are a magnificent little man."(Of course he understood that.)   The nurse informed me, "We have to go and get him ready for surgery. Dr. J. wants to do it right away."

So through the tears, I said what I hoped would not be the only words of encouragement and affection he would ever hear from me, "Be brave, my little son, and when this horrible ordeal is over and I can get up, I will come to the NICU and see you. I love you and I am proud of you, and if you can't make it back, it's okay. I'll see you in Heaven. I will be praying every minute." I kissed his cheek and he was gone.

That was a heck of a deal! It wasn't okay to just have one tearful encounter and then take him away to surgery, to danger. Nevertheless, okay or not, that was what happened. I prayed. I prayed for him. I prayed for peace. I prayed for strength. I was a wreck! I still cry about that night as I write this. It was unbelievably hard. My ears filled up with tears.

Things got worse. Dr. J. came and pulled up a stool beside my head because they were still sewing me up. Cody was going to surgery, and they were still sewing me up. I don't know much about fairness in this life, but I know a lot about unfair. That was not fair. I still remember Dr. J.'s words as if he said them just now. "The baby has the worst kind of spinal defect, a myelomeningocele. He is also 37 weeks gestation, so his lungs are immature. He has been intubated and put on the respirator and a central line is in place. Lots of things may happen. If his skin is not good around the defect, I may have to use wire and staples. He could lose a lot of blood. I may have to take him back to surgery several times tonight and tomorrow. He may not survive. If he does, he will probably be severely retarded. He will not be able to use the bathroom in a normal way. He will not be able to walk or run. He may never have sex."

At that point, I could take no more. "May never have sex? He is five minutes old! Do I have to deal with that now?"

He said calmly, "Momma, I have to tell you all of the truth so you can decide what you want to do."

I blurted out, "What do you mean what I 'want to do'?"

He explained, "Well, you can send him on to surgery with me tonight and see what happens or you can wait and get a second opinion or you can do nothing, and he will probably die within one week."

Most of the people who are constants in my life I have known for years, and I have felt very few moments of anger toward them at any time. I had known this man for about two hours, and I wanted to slap him. My baby was not a barbed wire fence in need of repair. I felt the courage rising, even in that most weak moment. I told him with conviction that we wanted to give him the best chance possible for a productive life and that I knew some marvelous handicapped people. I told him to go forward with surgery and to keep me posted. He said, "I must go and speak with your husband now, while they finish with you." I thought, *Go ahead, Buddy. You'll hear the same response from him. That, I am sure of.*

Then I asked with a desperate tone, "Dr. J., is there anything hopeful you can tell me?"

He replied, "The defect is low and the problems occur below the defect. Also, his head circumference, right now, is normal. That does not mean he will not have to have a shunt put in after I close his spine, but we will see."

My last question before he left was, "Do you think someday he might walk with braces and crutches?"

His response was, "Yes, that is probably a very realistic goal. I have to go now. You rest, and I will come and talk to you when the surgery is over."

I shouted as he walked out, "Take good care of our son. I will be praying for you and him and everyone in that operating room!" No response. He was out of there.

Well, there you go. His head circumference was normal; the defect was low. I needed something to cling to and that was all I could have at that moment. At a time when most parents are checking to see if their newborn has ten fingers and ten toes, I was left with news of ventilators and surgery and retardation and perhaps even death. The anesthesiologist said, "Honey, you are shaking so badly I need to give you a general anesthetic."

I exclaimed, "Oh, no. I have to be awake in case there are more decisions to be made about the baby tonight."

He said, "Then my other choice is to put these long boards under your arms and strap you down."

"Strap them down." I instructed, and he did it. At that moment, at that most horrible moment, I did something that most people just talk about. I stepped out on faith. I put Cody and us in God's hands, and again, God showed up!

Down the hall, far from me, Dr. J. had taken Paul into a room, not allowing any other family in, even at Paul's request. He told him basically the same things he told me, only with more negatives. Paul told me later how angry he had been, first at even the suggestion of letting our son lie in a crib and die. Paul said his response had been, "He is our baby, and just because he has a handicap, we are not going to throw him in the garbage." That was strong, but I thought, *Go Paul! Go Daddy!* After all, he had a new identity now too!

Then the talk worked its way into Dr. J. saying, "This will be hard. Many, many marriages break up; 85 percent of couples with handicapped children wind up divorced."

Paul stopped him there. Just as the "may never have sex" statement had been my limit, that was Paul's. He said he had responded with, "I think we are bigger than that."

When he was telling me this I said, "Go, Tiger."

Paul inquired, "Well, where did he read that statistic, in the Sports and Spokes magazine?" (That's a periodical on wheelchair sports.) "He is not a marriage counselor. I wanted to know about the baby." Again, I thought, *Go, Paul! Go, Daddy!* After that, Paul signed the consents for surgery and Dr. J. left. My mom and sister said when Paul came out of the room after the conference that he was as white as a sheet and trembling.

A lot of media attention was given at that time to "quality care" in hospitals. Some of our care was great, but I have to wonder why we could not be together when the doctor talked to us. We were not sequestered witnesses in a court trial, but it sure seemed like it. The separation just made one of the most difficult nights in our entire lives even more painful for both of us. In addition, the staff kept sending Paul down to the first floor to try and get a stamper card because the card-making machine was not working properly. Finally, Dr. J., who had already scared both of us to death, was taking Cody to surgery and saw Paul waiting for an elevator going down. He asked, "What are you doing?" Paul tried to explain and Dr. J. snatched the papers from Paul's hands saying, "Forget that, son. They have hospital employees to take care of that." He handed the papers to a nurse. Paul was relieved. As we would learn over the next seventeen years, Dr. J. is tough, but he does know how to take charge.

Paul was allowed to come in the surgery room where I was for a few minutes before they sent me to recovery. They were right; he was very pale and trembling. Of course, it probably did not help that he saw me with my arms straight out like an eagle's wings and strapped to boards with Velcro. The whole room was a disaster of trays and towels, Cody's resuscitation equipment was left behind too, not an inviting sight. Then there was his lovely wife, a wreck, looking like she was ready to be burned at the stake, shaking and crying. It had been a tough night, and it was not over. Never had I ever been so glad to see him—not to take me on any of our dates or even at the church for our wedding. We were shaky, but we were singing from the same page. Not much was said. He told me Cody was gone to surgery, but he had been able to get the nurse to stop on the way down the hall to let him and his sister peek into the isolette. He told me the baby was adorable, and he thought he looked like his daddy. He told me he loved me, kissed me on the forehead, and left because they said he had to.

That was a typical reaction for Paul. All the trouble surrounding the birth of our first child, and he was talking about how cute the baby was. I was glad he was not a medical person at that moment. I suffered fearing some terrible complications for our baby, complications that he was not aware could happen. In that way, he was blessed.

The next stop on my journey was the recovery room. What a lonely place. The only appearance of human life for the next two hours was a nurse, not too happy about being there at midnight, who took my vital signs, stated she knew nothing about what was happening with Cody, and left. Again, it was very cold on that stretcher, and if the hospital was striving for quality care, why was I left alone? Having that spinal, I was fully awake and frightened, but required to lie flat to prevent a spinal headache. My ears filled with tears again. Maybe they thought I needed a moment to myself. They should have asked.

I felt like I was spiraling down into a hole when I caught a glimpse of a young man in a white coat. I was sure it was one of our doctors, changed out of scrubs, coming to give me a report. As he got closer, I saw his handsome smile and he took my hand. It was not one of our doctors. It was my best friend's husband, who was a doctor, but not one of mine. When he and his wife were told they couldn't come back to recovery, he had gone to his car, gotten one of his lab coats and his nametag, and told them he was on my case. He was such a welcome sight, and when he told me what had happened, I told him he could be on our case any time. I am not sure how long he was there, but being a quiet man, I think my blubbering scared him. I am sure I clutched his hand harder and longer than he intended, but I needed some company and he was it. Shortly after he left, the nurse came back and told me as soon as I could feel my legs I could go where my family was. I longed to be with them. What a cruel situation! It was as if I had to earn the right to be with my family by regaining something I had no control over, and at a time when I needed to be with them so badly. I prayed for leg feeling.

During the time I was in recovery, I heard the phone ringing constantly. I remember, in among my flight of ideas, one of my thoughts was, *Whom are they calling for? No one else is here.* Later I heard one nurse say to the other one in disgust, "They are calling to check on that woman. She is friends with the nursing instructors, and they gave this private number out." At the time I thought, *They don't even know me and they don't like me.* Now I think that all of my supporters calling that number and Dr. E. posing as a member of our medical team is funny. Nurses should be careful about their reactions to patients' families and friends, especially during that type of crisis. Compassion needs to be an infinitely more important part of nursing than following the rules.

When I finally started feeling my legs, I wished I couldn't. The pain train had pulled into the station. Of course, they were running Pitocin (the labor-inducing drug) into my veins all night. I know it is necessary, but I kept thinking, *This is so unfair. Labor that does not hurt, a C-section, paralysis, and now labor that does hurt. God help me!*

I lost track of time but I don't remember sleeping at all. At some point, Dr. J. came to my room and told me the surgery had gone very well. Cody was in NICU on the ventilator, and he would see us later. I appreciated his coming to give me an update even though I knew he was tired. As the day shift came on, I made it my first order of business to see if they would stop the drug making me have those terrible contractions. The first nurse to come in was the nurse manager, the one I had asked to reroute Dr. J. the night before. She went to check on the orders and came back with this comment, "Bad news. He has ordered it for every bag of fluid."

"Bad news nothing! Call him up," I demanded. About that time, he appeared and ordered it stopped, but then he told me of the large bandage covering my incision. "There is only one way to do this." Then with one big jerk, he pulled off about fifteen inches of bandage and tape.

When I caught my breath, I remember telling him, "If I ever get up again, I am killing you." He must have been well conditioned to death threats because he laughed.

Then came the proverbial salt in the wound when he said, "I want you to get up this morning and walk to the bathroom."

I was in the greatest pain of my life. I looked at the three-foot distance to the bathroom and told him, "You come back at 8 P.M. and I will be in there." That would be twelve hours later. He laughed again and left. The laughter only lasted a moment, but it was a nice rest from crying.

CHAPTER 4

The Search for Hope

ALL THE WAY MY SAVIOR LEADS ME,
WHAT HAVE I TO ASK BESIDES?
CAN I DOUBT HIS TENDER MERCY,
WHO THROUGH LIFE HAS BEEN MY GUIDE?[24]

Fanny Crosby

That song takes on new meaning when you know that Fanny Crosby, the writer, was blind. She had to step out on faith when writing hundreds of hymns, including *Blessed Assurance,* and now so would we.

We had not fallen into the 15 percent for whom the ultrasounds were wrong. Somehow, I knew we wouldn't. Our baby was born with spina bifida. I still couldn't believe it, and I couldn't quit shaking. The day after delivery would prove to be very stressful and overwhelming.

All I could think of when Dr. H. left that morning after issuing the "walk to the bathroom" challenge was, *The blows just keep on coming.* What a nightmare! However, we didn't yet know what a nightmare was. We were about to find out.

Dr. H. and his nurse had only been gone for a few minutes when there was a knock at the door. Paul and I were the only ones in the room, and he was on a cot facing the wall. I thought he was asleep, and I was glad. After I invited the visitor in, a very attractive lady with a smile on her face entered. She verbally verified who I was, then introduced herself as the business manager of the NICU. Her next statement makes my blood run cold even as I write it here. It was as follows, in the most condescending tone I had ever heard, "If little Cody wants to stay in the NICU, he will need a $200 deposit."

I could *not* believe it! I was so dumbfounded the only reply I could muster was, "If you will look in that closet in my purse and hand me my checkbook and help me to hold my hand steady to protect my IV, I will write you a check." She did, thanked me for the money, and left.

Paul immediately sat up, and I asked him why he did not rescue me from her. He stated firmly, "If I had moved I would have punched her after what we just lived through last night, but I knew you wouldn't want me to have a confrontation with her so I didn't. I will be talking to the hospital administrator; you can bet on that." I wasn't able to punch anyone or fight with anyone, but I sure wish I had responded differently.

I wish I had told her, "Right now, all little Cody wants is to live. Send him to my hospital! I have insurance; you will get your money!" I could have even said, "That's *Mr.* Little Cody to you and the one who sent you to collect his fee!" Anything but writing that terrible, shaky check. What a horrible experience! Paul did talk to someone in administration before we were discharged, and he assured him that he would check into it. (Ten years later, a lady who had just had very premature twins who were not expected to survive, told us she had the same experience *with the same person.* My gosh! Somebody stop the madness!)

Soon after, my mom and sister came back into the room. I believe they had scattered to make phone calls. They were horrified when they heard the story. Everybody was exhausted. It was decided that my sister would stay with me while Paul went to check on his dad who was in a hospital across town receiving chemotherapy. Mom went home to bathe, change clothes, and prepare for whatever would come next.

When I told my sister about the bathroom walk order she said, "Well, you look exhausted. Why don't you get it over with? We will clean you up, get you something for pain, and maybe you can sleep." It sounded good, but it turned out to be a fiasco. I knew to sit up slowly, but I thought I was going to celebrate my next birthday before I was sitting. Once I was up though, I felt I could make it okay. I was wrong. Holding Cheryl's arm, I was able to slowly get to the bathroom and even sit, but painfully. I stayed there for a few minutes, and Cheryl's account of what happened next goes like this, "Raina called me into the bathroom and said she did not feel very well and would like to return to the bed. I gave her my arm, she stood up, what little color she had remaining suddenly left, and before I could do anything to prevent it, she fainted dead away on to the hard floor. Her head made a thud when it hit. I was horrified.

I called her name and she came to—almost immediately—and began pleading with me, 'Don't pull that thing! Please don't pull that thing.' I asked her loudly, being frightened and upset, 'What thing are you talking about?' She pointed to the emergency call button. So I didn't, and somehow I got her up without help and back in the bed. I vowed at that moment to never stay with her by myself again." She kept that vow. She only stayed with me after that if another family member or friend was there also. I hated that had happened, and I know I upset her. Still, fainted or not, I did not want half of the hospital personnel running in there to see what a mess I was in. I don't know if she really understood that, but nevertheless, she got me clean and settled, had the nurse give me a pain pill, and for a short while, I slept. Cheryl forgave me, I think, but that was the end of her private duty nursing.

The nurse manager who brought the pain pill happened to be my friend, and she asked how she could help me. After chewing me out for not calling her during the bathroom episode, I asked her if she would call the NICU and find out what Cody's ventilator settings were, because I was too scared to do so. She promised to check from the nurses' station. I was sure she was doing that in case the news was bad. I appreciated that.

She left the pain pill and went to call. She returned a few minutes later smiling. A very welcome sight that was, because as I had just proved, I already felt faint. "He is doing very well," she reported.

"What are his vent settings?" was my question.

Her answer was,"He is not on the vent, silly, that was just to go to surgery. His first x-ray of the chest was suspicious, but they said this morning's x-ray looks like a new baby."

I was so relieved. Off the vent! Praise God! My next question was, "What percent of oxygen is he getting in his oxyhood?"

She rolled her eyes and stated with conviction, "He is not on oxygen at all! You know too much! Go to sleep!" So I did.

Sleeping was very difficult on that crunchy hospital mattress, with all the noise, the pain, the dreams, and nightmares of all sorts. The phone kept ringing, and the flowers kept coming. Forty-seven arrangements before the day was gone. The little candy striper volunteers told me they had rounded up the last flower carts available in the hospital. I appreciated the love and concern; it buffered the crash a little, but I also detected an air of overcompensation. The people who loved us wanted to make this a happy time, and they hoped the flowers would help to do that. They probably would have individually, because later I was able to appreciate each message separately. Yet together they mocked flowers all arranged at a funeral, and it was scary. As I faded in and out of drug-induced sleep, I would see that wall of flowers, and I wasn't sure if I was laid out in the hospital or the funeral parlor.

That afternoon the nurse came and asked if I felt like going to NICU to see Cody. Was she kidding? Unlike the first try, I was out of the bed and into that wheelchair in record time. Paul pushed me down there. It seemed so strange to gown and wash my hands as I had instructed hundreds of visitors to do in my NICU. As we rounded the corner, it struck me how equipment intensive the NICU really is. Hospital survey-ors before had told me that and my thought was always, *Duh, it takes a lot of equipment to give intensive care, and you can't use it if it is in stor-age.* However, as a parent I could see what a frightening sight it was.

Cody was lying on his stomach, asleep, on a foam wedge so his head was downhill from the incision that the neurosurgeon created on his spine the night before. He had bilateral clubfeet; I could see that right away. In addition, there was an angry red square around the inci-sion. I realized two things when I saw it—my baby had the same type of bandage-jerking episode that morning that I had survived, and he was going to have skin that is easily irritated (which he does). He had an IV in his scalp, placed where his hair had been shaved, and I knew just at that moment how much that hurts. Parents had told me that for years, and I thought that was so silly because we have children's hair cut all the time, and it grows back. Right then I wanted something to remain intact. *What goes around really does come around.*

Paul walked right up to his bed, took his little hand, and started talking softly to him. That was the first time I had ever heard him even come close to whispering. I knew then that this child would bring changes in all of us. I had stood by the radiant warmers of so many babies that it was hard to grasp that this was my baby. I felt like I was in the twilight zone. I tried to talk to him, but all I could do was cry. I wanted to die, I wanted to go out of there, and so they took me back to my room. The first thing my waiting family and nurse asked me was, "Do you feel better now?" Were they crazy? I had never felt worse in my entire life.

My baby was so sick . . . and handicapped! Going to the NICU had only confirmed that, and I felt ill. I didn't talk to them because I knew they just wanted me to be okay. I just cried and prayed.

It is an awful thing when you are not really able to talk to the people you love but feel you have to. The phone kept ringing as I would tell the same story over and over, and the people and the flowers kept coming. My life is such an open book; the people closest to me never expect me to want to be alone. I wanted to be alone. I just wanted to scream at high volume for ten minutes, anything to relieve the pressure. I knew I couldn't. It would upset everyone too much. Maybe I should have, because the sequence that began that night was much more horrible than just screaming.

I was in too much pain to go to the next visiting time, or maybe I just couldn't face it. I wanted to see Cody, but I didn't want to have to pretend to everyone around me that I got comfort from our visits. I adored the baby, but I was in a panic about how we were going to manage our family now. I just wasn't willing to say it, because I did not want to hear everyone's opinion. As the day drew to a close, the walls and the darkness began to smother me. I was overwhelmingly convinced that I was dying. I began to scream, cry, and beg the nurse and my mom to do something, anything, to keep me from dying. They kept asking me, "Why do you think you are dying?"

I kept screaming, "I don't know, but I am." I didn't know. They call it post-partum depression. On the first night of it, after about two hours, they sedated me, and I eventually fell into a very troubled, deep sleep.

The second morning I awoke to someone whispering my name, holding my hand. It took a moment to focus, but when I did, I saw a beautiful young lady in pink scrubs and soon realized she was a dear friend of mine from high school. She was one of the charge nurses for NICU. I had forgotten she would be there. I was so glad to see her, but couldn't do anything but cry. She said, "It's okay. You don't have to talk; I just want to tell you something. This morning I went in and turned Cody over, and he has the sweetest little face I've ever seen, and with you as his momma, I know he will have a wonderful, full life." There you go, the first positive things said.

That same afternoon another nurse friend of mine came. She said to me, "Raina, you are going to hear all sorts of things from all kinds of people, but I tell you, the more normal you treat him the more normal he will be. I know, because my middle child has cerebral palsy."

True words of encouragement from both of them, greatly appreciated even all these years later. Priceless.

Cody progressed very well over the next two weeks, and his condition was upgraded rapidly. He moved through the stages of healing, moving from NICU to the step-down nursery, to rooming-in without difficulty.

My progression was not nearly as smooth. After three nights of screaming and crying and proclamation of my impending death, I begged the doctor to let me go home. I dreaded leaving Cody, but I just could not bear the hospital anymore. I was in the room on the end of the longest hall, which was the greatest distance from the nursery they could put me. The philosophy was to put me where I could not hear the newborns crying. That would have worked if they had stayed in the nursery, but they were in and out continuously to their moms and back to the nursery. Moreover, Cody wasn't dying, and I did not resent people with well babies. I was glad for their blessings of good health.

I guess situations like ours are hard on everyone, even the staff trained to care for post-partum patients and sick babies. Some of the NICU nurses were God-sent angels, and some were cold, rude, and even ignored us. My thoughts were, *What is up with that? Do they think it is my fault? Good grief, from what is known now, I am guilty of the big sin of having a folic acid deficiency (one of the B vitamins) and/or absorption problem. Are they upset because the neurosurgeon is hard on them, spina bifida babies are hard to take care of, because they know I run an NICU, or what?* More than likely the ones that ignored us just did not know how to handle it. What a shame that health-care workers in places like NICU are not always required to go to "handle it" school before becoming part of the staff. Moms who have experienced it will tell you that it is a terrible feeling to sit and hold your sick infant and cry in the presence of a hateful nurse, and even a more terrible fate to leave at the end of the visiting time knowing that person will be in charge of your infant's care for the next eight to twelve hours. Cody got excellent care, partly because of the high skill level of the NICU staff, partly because my good buddies were in charge positions, and partly because the rude nurses were only a couple out of many.

We were there at every visiting time to give him love and bonding. Still, we longed for the time of discharge. These were hard times for everyone involved. It was the tip of the iceberg, but we could not and did not focus on that. We felt that if we went home we could regroup and begin to feel normal again. In days to come, normal was a word we would delete from our vocabulary.

On the morning of Cody's fourth day of life, I was not doing well at all. My doctor decided to discharge me because Paul was such an attentive husband, and we would be going home to my mother's house. She was a medical technologist, and many of my friends were doctors and nurses. Everyone who witnessed the night psychosis thought going home might help.

No one on this earth can prepare a loving mother for separation from her child, even if the separation is temporary and visitation will be allowed several times each day. As my visit to the NICU ended that morning, there were plenty of reassuring efforts by everyone remaining with him that he would be well cared for. If they had cut my heart out, thrown it on the sidewalk, and stomped on it, it would not have been any more painful.

So many friends called me that morning. I guess they knew it would be difficult, but none of them could communicate with me because I was so choked. I tried to talk in between sobs, but nothing I said made any sense. I had the people who loved me the most and the nurses crying. It was a terrible morning. Sometimes situations, like questions on a standardized test, have no answer that seems completely right. That was one of those times, so we gathered all of our flowers and bears and balloons. They rolled me to the front drive of the hospital, and we left. I kept thinking death would feel better.

On the way home, I felt like I was on the edge of night. The cars were rushing by on the interstate, and I remember thinking, *Life rushes on whether you want it to or not.* I felt like I was going to jump out of my skin and those dang silver balloons kept popping together in the back seat. It is not more than six or seven miles from the hospital to my mom's house, but that morning it felt like sixty or seventy. Everyone was on edge.

When we came to our drive, there in our yard near the street was a sign that had been pounded into the ground, a sign shaped into a stork and painted with a diaper in his beak, a diaper holding a baby. The words were, "It's a Boy!" I was so touched. The tears flowed. Paul reached over and held my hand. He said, "I wish those could be tears of joy only."

I sobbed, "Me too." We both wondered how the best and most important event of our lives could have so much sadness associated with it. We relied on the only things we could, love and faith. That got us through.

I was so thankful we could go to my mom's house. We live just across a driveway, but right then I could not face the bassinette, mobile, baby clothes—not yet.

Being there was better, but not nearly as much as I had hoped. The first thing I wanted to do when we were settled in the guest room was call the NICU and check on Cody. The nurses assured me he was fine, and although I was welcome to call anytime, it would be better if I rested. Resting was almost impossible. We had delivered our first child in turmoil. He was not only very sick and in danger, but he also had a permanent disability that affected many of his systems. On top of that, we had been required to leave him in the NICU while we came home. I longed for my early days of pregnancy when my biggest burdens were morning sickness, selecting a name, arranging childcare for when I returned to work, and how to decorate the nursery. I had been on top of the world. Now I had to remind myself to breathe.

I prayed, I cried, I read scriptures, I talked with people who loved me, and I experienced what I felt was numbness and shock. I kept praying, "Lord, how do I get past this? I don't even feel human."

The first snap back to reality was getting ready to get back in the car and drive to that hospital for the afternoon NICU visit. Why hadn't I just stayed there? Nevertheless, I couldn't; I was going crazy. No good answers were flowing to anything. I decided to take a bath and wash my hair. I sat in a chair and used the blow dryer. I felt a little refreshed. When I was ready, my mom, bless her heart, had prepared a beautiful lunch of all of my favorite foods, complete with tablecloth, centerpiece, good china, the works. The whole family and a few close friends were there. Before we sat down to eat, as is tradition in her home, Mom had everyone hold hands, and she said a prayer of thanks for all of our blessings, hope for Cody's health, and blessed the food. I felt my throat tighten. As the tears flowed, I came to a difficult realization that holds true today. The grief caused by the handicapping of a child will sit as a lump in your throat for the rest of your life. No matter how old they get or how well they do, it just never really goes away.

I managed to eat a little, and I still remember how wonderful everything tasted. I was spoiled by my mom's fabulous cooking. Between being upset and the history of industrial food, I had not let anyone around me even remove the lids from the hospital food. I was ill, but after three days of not eating, I was a wee bit hungry. I could not yet really follow normal conversation—too much "flight of ideas", but for the moment, the love I felt in that room gave me hope for "life after post-partum blues."

Paul and I went alone to our first visit from home to the NICU. He talked without ceasing—bubbling over about the baby, how glad he was I was home, how his mom and dad and grandmother had been impressed when they went to see and pray for Cody, and about tapes and programs he had watched with happy, productive physically-challenged children as the stars. I was weak and full of dread and I remember thinking, *I hope he is not making all of that up to make me feel better.* I wanted to place hope in what he was saying since he seemed to have done so, but all the trauma of the last month, especially the last few days, had knocked the legs out from under me. Fear and dread held on.

Actually, my mom had gone to see Cody during the allowed time before we arrived because I had only been home for two hours. It was decided that she could go that five miles for the allotted twenty-minute visit in our place that one time. You might know, she met up with the orthopedic doctor for the first time. That really upset me. The one time I wasn't there, someone so important to Cody's course was there. If I had known how many hours and traumas he would see us through in Cody's life, I would not have given it a second thought. She told me he had given her new hope, and he was impressed with Cody's leg strength and movement. He had talked of a course of many surgeries, but Cody was unusually strong for that point and with the type of defect he had. I was desperate for all the good news I could hear.

On our visit, the NICU nurses reported that same assessment.

On top of that, we got to hold Cody, feed him, rock him, talk to him, and sing to him. He was awake the whole visit and watched every move we made. He looked better, he was less irritable, he was moving his legs, and he seemed bright. I knew there were severe problems, but hope was building.

The nurses also told of the urologist's visit and what a caring doctor he was. In my mind, the idea of a team concept was being planted. Little did I know that along the way we would grow a huge team of doctors, nurses, therapists, social workers, receptionists, teachers, coaches, medical supply people, and a whole host of new friends. We began to understand that raising this child was going to be quite an adventure. It already had been, and we were barely getting started. Leaving him was still hard, but it had been a good visit.

So we began a daily routine of traveling back and forth from my mom's house to the hospital's NICU, three times a day, to visit Cody. He looked better every day, as we bonded more and more with him. There were controversies and mixed emotions at times. Some people said he moved his toes and some said he could not. Very often throughout his life there have been issues that were left to the interpretation of the doctors, the nurses, the family members, the therapists, etc., and those became the most difficult issues, the ones you toss and turn over all through the night. Many times I have read the serenity prayer when seeking guidance. The one that says:

Lord, give me the serenity to accept the things I cannot change, the courage to change the things I can, and the wisdom to know the difference.[5]

It is a beautiful prayer, and wisdom is such a wonderful virtue, but with spina bifida, sometimes you can go all the way up the food chain and never find anyone who has the wisdom to know the difference between what you can and cannot change. I suppose a lot of things in life are like that, where all the uncertainty causes you to lose a lot of sleep unnecessarily, and all you ever accomplish is losing sleep.

For one week after going home the night psychosis/anxiety attacks continued. I can still see Paul with a pillow over his head (to block the brightness of the overhead light) asking, "When do you think you can go to a night light?"

By the end of my first week at home after Cody's birth, the anxiety attacks were subsiding. I had come to the realization that if I were dying each night, ten days after delivery, I would be dead already. No rocket science there. I was able to reduce the lighting in the room at night to one small lamp, for which Paul was thankful. Cody was moved to the step-down nursery, for which the whole family was thankful. All the trips back and forth to the hospital caused my C-section incision to open and drain a ridiculous amount. Antibiotics were ordered. At the time I thought, *The hits just keep on coming.* Now I believe it was all tolerance and persistence training for the many setbacks and complications we would experience in Cody's life. I had not been psychotic, just lost. Little by little, I was coming around.

The next adventure began when I arrived at the hospital on the morning of about the eleventh day, and the nurses said the neurosurgeon was waiting in a conference room to talk to me. I told them, "I'm scared of that." They laughed. In reality, I was very scared and weak. I was pleasantly surprised when he wanted to tell me it was time for me to move back into a room on the OB unit and have Cody room-in with me for three days in preparation for his discharge. Paul had returned to work because the Family Medical Leave Act had not yet been set in motion, but he would be there in the evenings and at night.

I was so excited! Discharge! That meant we could take our baby home. He had survived a terrible ordeal, but all is well that ends well. Right?

On the golden opportunities when I am privileged to speak to parents of disabled children now, I caution them about moments like that. Hope is so important for survival but so is keying in on words like *permanently* in phrases like "permanently disabled." The story only ends when their lives end. The key is to brace yourself for a lifetime of crises in the back of your mind but take only one at a time in your foremost thoughts. That is a very difficult task. That is where faith and the ones who love you are your tools for survival.

The ones who love me could hardly contain me. I could not get things packed quickly enough. Most of that was so unnecessary and cumbersome, but I was being pampered during that period, so nobody argued with me. One of Paul's famous sayings is, "If you want to pack like Raina, take everything you own and put it in every suitcase you have, and you will be there." He is such a know-it-all. The sad part is . . . he is almost right. How dumb, my incision was already not healing well. Yet for the moment, I felt I needed lots of clothes and supplies to be sure Cody was well cared for.

Back then they must have put rooming-in mothers in the reject rooms of the hospital. I was taken to the ugliest room I had ever seen, with a fantastic view of some huge air units. However, it all became so *not* important the moment they rolled that crib with my little son in and put him in my arms. I thought, *Oh my God, I have waited and wished for this moment all of my life. Thank you, Lord. We are so blessed.* Paul and I both cried. We were finally a real family. I knew in that moment we would survive. We had to because he was too precious not to. One of the real secrets to doing well with handicapped children is to make the most of the good times and not dwell on or mire up in the bad. We sure made the most of that one, with pictures too. It was a real "Kodak moment."

The joy was there, but soon boredom would arrive. I never expected that. Paul had to go back to work. Cody and I were alone. My friends were afraid to call much for fear of waking him or intruding on a precious moment for the two of us. On top of that, there was a charge, an unreasonable charge, to turn the TV on, so I refused. Many people offered to pay it, but I said no on principle. I am not a cheapskate, but let's get real. Why would you put a mother who has had a difficult time and is trying to recover in an "ugly award" room for a three-day stay with a newborn who will be sleeping 75 percent of the time—then charge her a fee twice the price of going to a movie each day for an already-existing TV service in a not-for-profit facility? Give me a break! I lived without it. I treasured the moments Cody was awake, but he slept except during feedings and for a few moments afterwards. I was afraid at the time that the "may be severely retarded" phrase Dr. J. had warned me about at birth was going to be a reality. Now I realize the child was just exhausted from his ordeal and was finally in a quiet place with his mom where he could rest. Back then, my thoughts cost me many wasted tears. Along the way, I tried to apply to my life a saying that goes like this:

From all the sayings in this world, This one's tried and true;
Never trouble trouble, until trouble troubles you.[6]

That's a very difficult lesson I am still trying to live by all these years later.

On the morning of the second day, a nurse came to give me the agenda for the day. I had been told that she had spent several years as an RN working in a hospital for disabled children and taking care of many spina bifida kids. I was excited when I saw her, because I believed she would give me some real enlightening and positive information. I needed that because I knew then as I do now that the future is hope. My conversation with her turned out to be one of the most negative parts of rooming-in. Some people are just hard to figure out.

She introduced herself with minimal courtesy, which was a great disappointment. (I was hoping a nurse with a background of work with disabled kids, who now worked with rooming-in moms and new-borns, would be kind and friendly). She began the conversation with a regimented schedule. I immediately tried to turn the conversation to her experiences with spina bifida children. All she said was, "Those kids were amazing. They would jump out of bed in the mornings early, catheterize themselves, put on their braces, and be out in the playroom before I could start my day."

Completely absorbed in what she said and longing for more stories I inquired, "Not all of them had to catheterize did they?" As an RN, I know she could hear my desperate plea for hope.

She snapped back, "Of course all of them had to catheterize, and I tell you something lady, you are not going to get any of us to tell you he is going to be okay." I was crushed. That lady knew a lot of helpful, hopeful things she could have shared at a time when we were desperate for that, but she chose to be negative and cruel. Why? I was not asking for a written guarantee. I just needed some encouragement from some-one who was familiar with spina bifida and the course it runs. Nothing positive was going to come from her. I had no more questions. I sat and listened to her agenda without comment. I wanted her to leave and she did. No apology, no positive remarks. What a shame she was allowed to work in either place. After she left, Cody woke up crying. As I fed and rocked him, I promised him and myself that we would never adopt her attitude. In fact, we would not spend one minute more than was required in the presence of people with that kind of attitude. I could not help but wonder what the purpose of rooming-in really was. I had been feeding and changing babies with birth defects for years.

That afternoon when Paul arrived, he and I were scheduled to go to CPR class. I was an instructor, but when they told me everyone was treated the same, I did not argue. When the nurse came in to take Cody to the nursery so we could go to the classroom, she asked if we would take some extra gift packs because they had not had as many babies that month as they had anticipated. Since those packs had diaper coupons, etc., in them, we agreed. She said they would put them in the closet of my room while we were gone.

As soon as we got in the classroom, both the instructor and I realized that I had taught her CPR. We were both embarrassed. We tried to joke about it, but after the cruelty of the morning nurse and now taking CPR from one of my students, I was growing very weary of following the program. However, since my feelings had been hurt that morning, I was not about to hurt hers. Therefore, I was cooperative. Besides, it meant I did not have to scare Paul half to death teaching him infant CPR. They did it for me.

To finish off a lovely day, when we returned to the room, we discovered 50 gift packs in that closet. What a mess!

Paul and I were adjusting well to Cody's needs, and he was so content with us. That was the good part. The three of us spent some precious time together until Cody was asleep for the night, then Paul gathered as many of the gift packs as he could carry, kissed me goodnight, and headed home. That familiar night panic started to take over, but I fought it off with prayer and concentrating on the fact that in one more day we would finally be able to take our baby home. I slowly fell into an exhausted sleep.

The next morning, right after Cody's feeding and after several phone calls, a nurse appeared. She was much friendlier than the nurse the day before, but I had not slept much. When she revealed the fact that she was a new LPN graduate there to teach me how to give Cody a bath, I came unglued. I had no desire to hurt her feelings, but enough was enough. I asked her to go get the charge nurse, after reassuring her that she had done nothing wrong. She left and returned moments later with the charge nurse in tow. I explained to both of them that I was exhausted, my incision was draining like a cracked water hose, and I was fully capable of giving Cody a bath and any other care he needed at home. I kindly insisted of the charge nurse that Dr. J., the neurosurgeon, be paged. Her answer was, "He does not want any of us telling him anything about anything." She chuckled. I was not in a laughing mood.

What I shared with her was, "I know nobody looks at it this way, but I hired him to take care of my son. Please page him." So she did. One hour later he and his nurse arrived. My plea was, "I want to take Cody home, please. If I have any trouble giving him a bath, I'll call you."

He knew my background and my present problems, and he responded, "Okay, Momma. Okay."

He wrote the orders and talked as he did. He told me not to be discouraged because when he was little, his feet were clubbed just like Cody's feet were. I asked him, "What did they do to straighten them out?"

He explained, "The only thing they knew to do in the old country—my grandmother strapped cardboard to both of my feet until they straightened." I was a little unsure about that story but appreciated the word of encouragement anyway. He only gave me two sentences of instructions. We were to bring Cody to his office on the next Monday morning, only six days after discharge, and to call him if we needed any medical assistance. I was so relieved. I had expected an hour-long lecture. He did add, as he left the room, to keep Cody away from people because visitors would bring a risk of infection and that would be dangerous. I was so excited! I called Paul and told him to come quickly and take us home before they could change their minds. Everything we needed for the trip home was already there. He said he was on his way.

Before Paul could arrive, the nurse came in with discharge instructions. Another happy moment turned sour. She presented me with a list of fifteen to twenty places, doctor's offices, etc. I would need to call over the next few days to make appointments. My heart sank. How on earth was I ever going to manage? The tears flowed. Where were the people from social services, public relations, anybody? I needed help! What a depressing and overwhelming moment! If only someone . . . that nurse, Dr. J., or any one of the health-care team had just told me to take it easy, to take it one issue at a time. If they had given me a hint of all the wonderful helpers I would have in Cody's life, I would have a different memory. That is why, when I make presentations to nursing students, I encourage them, "Don't leave moms hanging. Go the extra mile. Make a few phone calls. Help them set priorities. Give words of encouragement. Treat them as you would want to be treated. After all, isn't that what nursing is? Taking care of people." Knowing Dr. J. as I do now, I know he would have insisted on that if he had known they were going to leave all of it for me to do.

I felt alone and frightened. Cody woke up and I snapped out of it. "Come on, Son," I said lifting him into my arms. "Let's put on your going-home clothes, because, Hallelujah, we are going home!" I dressed him in a precious blue and white outfit I had bought for his going-home clothes before we knew about the spina bifida. With all the change of plans we had encountered, it was still the same—one of the few "normal" things we got to do.

Paul and the nurse assistant arrived, and we loaded our belongings on a cart. Paul made some comment about hauling out 65 flower and balloon arrangements on the first trip, and now it was 50 gift packs and the trainload of clothes and supplies I had collected. I didn't care; we were headed home with our baby, and he looked adorable, even if one side of his head was shaved and bruised from IV's. After thanking everyone, he and I were required to be rolled down in a wheelchair as if I had never been home. That was crazy, but I thought, *Nothing else is going to upset me today.* Wrong.

After we were in the car, which Paul had parked right in the front drive of the hospital, he turned and proclaimed, "I have to tell you something I have been putting off saying. It has to be said before we leave here." What a terrifying moment. I thought, *Is he going to leave home? Is it too much for him? What on earth is wrong?* He looked so sad.

With a trembling voice, I instructed him, "Okay, say it." I would not tell him I was ready because I felt I wasn't, but we could not sit there all day.

Softly, he shared with me, "I can't change diapers with poop in them." Was he nuts? Scaring me to death over that? Good grief! Thank goodness, I looked at him and realized he wasn't kidding.

Instead of knocking him out of the car, I just blurted out, "You'll be over that by tomorrow. Let's go."

So we left. We journeyed toward home with all of our hopes and doubts and fears, our long list of appointments to make with doctors, therapies, and follow-up exams, and our sweet little son, asleep in the car seat as if he felt assured Mom and Dad would take care of everything.

CHAPTER 5

Cody's Home—Let's Set Our Goals

*FOR EVERYTHING YOU HAVE MISSED,
YOU HAVE GAINED SOMETHING ELSE.*[7]

Ralph Waldo Emerson

When we arrived home this time, we did go to our house. Cody's first fan club was waiting, and they were a little disappointed that he continued to sleep. We sat the infant carrier he was in on top of the bassinet mattress. The bassinet was in the den where everyone had gathered. In his beautiful little blue and white outfit, including socks and shoes, with his head turned where the shaved portion of his scalp was concealed, he looked as adorable and normal as any newborn.

The family and friends there had comments that fed into that illusion. Those are moments you cherish but must be cautious with. Otherwise, without truly facing reality, you can never lead a handicapped child down the path that is best, and unfortunately, some don't. We were praying some of the negatives we had been told to face would not happen, and they have not. Yet by facing the limitations he does have, we hoped then and still hope today to be able to help him to make a difficult, yet marvelous journey. A journey, a pilgrimage, which does not concentrate on ignoring his limitations, but rather on finding and developing his abilities.

We all have limitations, and we all have gifts. In ancient times there was a prayer used by inns for "The Stranger Within Our Gates." Part of it read, "We are all travelers. From birth till death we travel between the eternities. May these days be pleasant for you, profitable for society, helpful for those you meet, and a joy to those who know and love you best." As I looked at my little son sleeping there, I thought of that prayer and the words John Denver sang, "I am looking for my family and all of you are mine."[8]

I was not sure how disabled he would be, what his personality and abilities would be, how we would manage physically, emotionally, and financially. At that moment, I was only sure of one thing—God loves us. He does not leave us alone, and He had given us a mission. I vowed at that moment to be the team leader, to be truly committed to use what abilities I had to lead us down the path that was best for Cody, no matter how difficult, how exhausting, or how sad. We would never quit. So many times in life we are wandering around lost, not sure what we are supposed to be doing. That was not one of those times. I had no assurance of what could lie ahead, but with God and the help of our family and friends, I knew we could conquer it. That little baby, sleeping so sweetly, was about to take us on a roller coaster ride no theme park in America could match. It would turn out to be the greatest joy and the biggest job of my life.

Getting organized and setting priorities and goals for Cody's care were extremely difficult. Almost every day for the first few weeks, I was sitting in the waiting room of a doctor's office. Patience had not been my greatest virtue before, but it would have to be now. My days were doctor's visits, tests, therapy, etc., sometimes hearing many negatives. Evenings were family time, trying to find the cuteness, the hope of a good life. Nights were when I would put him to bed and get in the tub to cry and grieve and try to disseminate the information obtained from the health-care team that day. My life was pressure beyond belief. I was not healed from the C-section, not healed emotionally, and everyone in our lives wanted to take us in a different direction. At night my head would reel like a never-ending power point set on a three-second timer. I slept very little, and if the bathtub had not had a drain, it would have floated down the street in a river of tears.

I began to hear from so many, "I couldn't do it. That's why God gives special kids to special people." What a cop out! When you consider the parents of some handicapped children, believe me, there is nothing special about them. Moreover, to me, all kids are special. However, I was beginning to realize a few things that would direct our lives. The first was that we would have to pick and choose his course from many, many choices—what doctors we would see and how much of each one's directions we would follow. The same would be true of choosing extra-curricular activities, therapies, surgeries, etc. There is no book of instructions for raising any child. However, for one with disabilities, you are really the captain of your ship, often without an experienced navigator, or even worse, with the wrong navigator. Scary, but little by little, we set our course and latched on to those who had the resources to help us to survive: the doctors and nurses on his team, Special Children's Services, and the family and friends who were willing and able to make the journey. Unfortunately, where family was concerned, the numbers were very small. Where friends were concerned, not every one you expect to offer support can handle the emotion of it. Two incidents stick out in my mind. One is about a family member and one about a friend.

My only sister, the one who had been with me for the fainting spell the day after Cody was born, was waiting with the fan club when we arrived home. She was excited to see him, but I noticed that she never held him. She would often sit beside whoever was holding him, but she would make an excuse if they tried to give him to her. At first, Paul and I had our feelings hurt. It seemed like rejection, but I soon realized it was fear. She was in denial, but I knew from our conversations she was afraid of harming his back or hips. No degree of reassurance that his back was closed and that he would not break did any good.

One day I looked out the kitchen window that faces the pool at her house, and I saw her sitting in a poolside chair that was very low to the ground. I had an idea. I put a one-piece outfit on Cody, a hat, no socks or shoes, sunscreen, and I walked over to where she was. I said, "Here, hold him for me while I go in and talk to Mom." I quickly placed him in her arms and left before she could either rise and escape or make an excuse. I stayed inside for two hours, peeping out occasionally when she wasn't looking to make sure he was happy. When I emerged two hours later with a bottle, she wanted to feed him, so I let her. From that day on, they have been big buddies.

I also had a nurse friend to whom I was very close. We had helped each other through crises for years. We knew each other's families well. We had a lot of fun throughout the years, called and visited each other often, and never had any misunderstandings. She was a wonderful person, and I loved being friends with her because she is twenty years my senior and knowledgeable about many things I had not yet experienced.

I thought after Cody was born that she would be right there with me in the crises. Oddly enough, she began to distance herself. Years later she would come to see us and tell me that she had thought of us and prayed for us every day. She exclaimed, "I just could not handle it! I still can't."

I wanted to hug her and say, "It's okay, forget it," but it wasn't okay, and I had not been able to forget it. So I said nothing. I had a hunch that if I let her continue she would be relieved of something she very much needed to say, and I very much needed to hear. My hunch was right. She confided, "When Cody was born, I could not believe that happened to you. I had to move away from it. It was too hard and only through the growth in my faith can I come here now. I couldn't call or come or write. Cody is charming. (He was ten years old then.) I am ashamed. I know you don't understand because we always encouraged each other through crises. Even now, it is too hard." I thought she was going to break and run. She couldn't even look at me.

This is what I shared with her, "If you are asking for forgiveness, you have it. Still, I would be an idiot to stand here and tell you I wasn't hurt or that I understand, but we are all different. Not being able to count on some of the people closest to me was extremely hard. However, God showed up, sometimes in the most unexpected people and places. Cody is a precious child; I am sorry his handicap kept you from knowing that."

What Cody and I learned along the way was that so many people are not equipped to handle crises. They have the background to be able, but they aren't. We have often found that our bad situations were more difficult for others to handle than for us. Weird, but true. Whatever we needed to survive, we had. We had the strength to do so, head on, but many, even those we hold dear, do not have as much courage and faith. Many face adversity with silence, avoidance, and distance.

The other lesson we learned was that, "You find out who your friends really are," is not always true. Don't think it will be your dearest friend who will come and load that wheelchair in the car and take your child on a fun day out. Instead, it will be someone you did not realize cared so much. When Cody was little, a friend of Ma's who worked with her and had a child Cody's age would come and take him shopping and out to eat. Myra and Bart became welcomed friends. So did Sherry, who also worked with Ma. She became one of the "older women" Cody had a crush on, because she had no problem taking him to ballgames, craw-fish boils, etc. They both had big hearts.

Once a quiet, shy friend of Paul's, who was a fireman, visited during one of Cody's confinements to the hospital. It was on a morning when Cody and I were the only ones there. After the departure of that friend, who had stayed three hours and had only a few strained words of conversation, I was thinking how strange and uncomfortable his visit had been. A few moments later I opened the bedside table drawer to discover a one hundred dollar bill lying there. There was no note accompanying the money. No note was necessary. Those are the type of deeds that really give life meaning. Some of your most faithful prayer partners will never tell you about their prayers, and some of the constant callers just want to know the scoop. Blanket judgments can cost you some of the dearest friendships of your life. We tried to avoid them.

Over the next few months, Cody began to develop what would become a life-long ability of charming people. Paul and I, along with my mother and sister and his family, began to do everything we could to stimulate him. Every week the message from the neurosurgeon was the same. He would look at his CT scans, measure his head, and deliver this report, "His head continues to grow above the normal curve and his ventricles are dilated. He will be severely retarded. Face it, accept it, that's how it will be." I always left his office crying. He was a brilliant doctor and we trusted him, but he always made me cry. The orthopedic doctor, urologist, and pediatrician were also great doctors. Even though they were not as negative, they let me know it would take a lot of therapy and many surgeries before he would walk or be able to function beyond infancy. It was overwhelming.

I had gone back to work when Cody was three months old. My sister-in-law and mother-in-law had agreed to keep him while I worked. Everyone else in the family worked also, but it was too much to ask of everyone. I was trying to supervise the NICU, and it was just too hard. One afternoon my mother-in-law met me at the door when I arrived to pick Cody up to tell me what I had feared. They just could not manage him. She was right, but I was devastated. What was I going to do? The doctors had been very adamant about not putting him in day care. We agreed. The risks were too great, and besides, we were beginning to discover what narrow-mindedness and prejudice were all about. I had called some day cares and some day care directors, even church day cares, but they had the same attitude, "We will pray for you, but we don't have the training to keep a child like him."

My statement was always the same. "We thank you for the prayers, but we have an army of people praying for him. What we need is child care." After several of those calls, I felt sick.

We got so tired of being treated like second-class citizens because our child had a disability. I picked Cody up and he smiled so sweetly. He was in a pavloc harness, a strap device to keep his legs bent like a frog's in an attempt to put his displaced hips back in the sockets without surgery. The harness had a couple of straps that had to be undone and re-buckled when changing his diaper, but how hard was that? All of the family had learned to do the whole process in less than five minutes. Other than that, he had to be fed and burped and rocked and put down for a nap just like any other infant. Our bond was strong, and as upset as I was, he was smiling. So I said this, "That's okay, Buddy. God will make a way, and some day the people that would not help us will wish they had been part of your life." I'm not sure if that is true. We have made so many detours since then I don't even know who the people were that rejected us, but I can't think of anyone who has been a part of our lives that is sorry to have met Cody.

So I went home and told Paul and the rest of my family we had no one to keep Cody. We all had to work just to stay afloat. We decided to make a list of our options. When we went to bed that night, a blank piece of paper lay on the dining room table. I prayed, "Lord, send the answer to child care. Safe, loving child care." Then I cried myself to sleep. By then I was used to sleeping on a tear-soaked pillow.

The next morning I awoke to my four-month-old, jabbering son, and I knew the answer. I would ask for a temporary demotion, work forty-hour weekends, and Paul and I would trade up and do the majority of the childcare ourselves. After all, I was struggling trying to work the normal 8 A.M.-4:30 P.M., Monday through Friday, head nurse hours and get him to all of his appointments anyway. I knew it would be like working seven days a week. I knew it would be hard on our marriage. It still seemed like the right answer. When Paul awoke, I told him. Now most men would have been concerned about not having enough time together. Paul was not like most men. Paul wanted to try it because it would be best for Cody. He and Cody, "my boys" as I still call them, would both prove to be extraordinary.

The first thing I did when I arrived at the hospital that morning was call the office of the Director of Nurses and asked for a conference. I had long since learned to run the NICU smoothly, so when I called she was immediately alarmed. She agreed to a meeting right away, and when I presented my proposal, she was stunned. "You have worked so hard to get where you are. Isn't there any other way?" She began to cry and so did I. She had been a nursing instructor at the university when I was a student there, so we were very close.

When I regained my composure, I told her this, "Asking for a demotion is difficult for me, especially from a position I worked hard to be promoted into, but to tell you the truth, I can no longer do it justice anyway. I hate not doing my best. I am often late, which you and some of my closest peers have been upset about. You hate to say anything because of my situation, but I hear rumblings. In some ways, it will be a relief. The pressure is too much, and Cody has to be priority." Due to making after work appointments and having to rise at 5 A.M. every morning to do all of his care and get everything he needed for the day, dropping him off before work and picking him up after work, home activities, plus calls and beeps from the staff, I was doing twenty-hour days. I am not just a whiny person.

She knew that, and after enlightening her that morning, I believe she was upset that she had not already realized what I was dealing with. She promised to start the paper work that day, ask the other "head nurse material" RN if she would assume the position, and change my schedule. I thanked her sincerely and promised to reconsider when our situation improved. We hugged and I left.

That was a very difficult morning, but things were going to work out. I would be with Cody four days a week without the burdens of my job looming over me. What a relief! That was one of the many times when what seemed like the worst thing that could possibly happen turned out to send us in a truly positive direction. "When God closes a door He opens a window."[9] It's true.

> *Some keep the Sabbath going to church;*
> *I keep it staying at home,*
> *With a bobolink for a chorister,*
> *And an orchard for a dome.*
> *Some keep the Sabbath in surplice;*
> *I just wear my wings,*
> *And instead of tolling the bell for church,*
> *Our little sexton sings.*
> *God preaches, -a noted clergyman,-*
> *And the sermon is never long;*
> *So instead of getting to Heaven at last,*
> *I'm going all along!*[10]

After that, I became a stay-at-home mom the first four days of every week and worked like a Trojan in the NICU the other three while Paul was Mr. Mom. We had to pretty much give up going to church on Sunday. I hated that, but I knew God was with us. Our faith was the strongest it had ever been. The best thing was the quality time we spent with Cody. We often went to the park and the zoo. We lay on a quilt under this huge oak tree with the sun filtering through the leaves, and he would jabber and giggle. We rode down the incline in our backyard in a red wagon. We read books and sang. I never had to worry about him being mistreated when I was working. Paul had gone from an "I can't change diapers with poop in them" dad to the most doting father any-where. Friends would tell me they saw them at the zoo or park or mall when I was working. I was so thankful for his dedication to his family. When he was working, I tried to be just as dedicated in between the medical tasks.

At five months Cody said his first word . . ."mote," then "want mote." He was referring to the TV remote control. All I could think about was Dr. J.'s words of, "No normal intelligence, no normal life expectancy." I thought, *Okay, Pal, I get it. No normal anything.* How many babies are there in the world whose first word is not "da da" or "momma," but "mote"? He was a monkey with a disability.

Cody became a patient of Special Children's Services. On our appointment days there, we were asked to be there at 6:30 A.M. We would check in and the first doctor would arrive between 8:30 A.M. and 9 A.M. By the time, all four doctors saw us it would be 2–3 P.M. Then we were sent to the office of one of the social workers, but at least they would assist in arranging for tests and braces and therapies. They were so much more helpful and friendly than the hospital personnel had been upon discharge. As a matter of fact, the only negative experience with our social worker was on our first visit after Cody became a patient there. J.C. was telling me how cute and active and bright she found Cody to be. I thanked her and said, "Thank God we made it through the big hospital crisis and moved on."

Her face fell and she replied, "You did, but just remember, that is the first crisis of many, many you will encounter." I was appalled. Why did everyone feel obligated to point out the negatives? I had very harsh feelings toward her at that moment. She could see that. I know my silence was deafening. She did not recant nor apologize. We left as soon as our appointments were scheduled. Cody fell asleep as soon as we started home, and I wept. It was becoming increasingly difficult to make myself take him to see those negative people.

But over the years, those negative people became very dear to my heart, and I developed an understanding of the therapeutic value in pointing out negatives to the mother of a child with a permanent disability, even when that child was still an infant.

The deal is, as with any difficulty in life, you can only begin to find hope and direction and solutions when you leave denial behind. The first stage of grief is denial, and your child does not have to be dying for you to grieve. You just can't solve any problem until you admit there is a problem. J.C. knew my well-being and Cody's was in danger if I did not brace us for the rough ride ahead, if I believed I had left hard times back at the hospital on discharge. I was to go back years later and thank her for making the statement I was so upset about that day. Life takes some funny turns.

Special Children's Services was our primary source of health care for a couple of years, until money parameters released them from

providing services to us. What a joke! You would have to be a million-
aire not to need help with a spina bifida child. During the two years they
were such a part of our lives, three particular incidents are prominent in
my memory.

The first was when Cody was six months old. Times were hard.
Paul's father had just passed away from cancer, and Paul was finishing
his degree at the university, working, and pulling his duty with Cody.
Money was tight. One morning, the next day after one of my forty-hour
weekends, I rose at 5 A.M. to dress Cody in clothes and harness and be at
our appointment at 6:30 A.M. across town. I had also put on him a bright
yellow jacket with a drawstring hood. It was a favorite. It was a cold and
rainy winter morning. With great difficulty, I managed to get Cody in
the car seat from under an umbrella in the freezing rain. I loaded all of
our supplies needed to spend the day there, got in the driver's seat, put
the wet umbrella in the back, and started out. The rain was heavy; the
cold was bitter. The heater was slow to warm. Just as I made it to the end
of our street, the car stalled. I was so scared. I knew if we did not get off
that road, someone would hit us. At that time, except for my family, all
the people on our street were elderly. There were no cell phones then.
Paul had gone to work. We were going to be late and be moved to the
bottom of the list. Somehow, I got out in the freezing rain and pushed
that car off the road. I got back in and began to cry.

I wanted to have a pity party. I looked over at Cody strapped in
that harness and buckled in that car seat in a freezing car with a sobbing mother and from under that yellow drawstring hood was a beaming
smile. I knew from that moment on who was helping whom to survive.
In the next moment, from out of nowhere, a young man in a raincoat
was tapping on my window. I nearly jumped out of my skin. He said,
"Ma'am, do you need help? My truck has the ability to tow." He towed
us home. Paul came and took us to our appointment. We were not even
late. When asked, the man told me his name and what company he
worked for. Neither one was listed in the phone book. I asked many people over many months. No one knew him, no one saw him that morning,
and the company was well known but did not have an office listed in our
town. Angels among us; forget explaining it.

The most outstanding occurrence during our time with Special
Children's Services happened one day when Cody was seven months

old. He had been wearing the pavloc harness to keep his hips in socket almost since he was born. We had already corrected his bilateral clubfeet with tiny casts. They had been recasted two or three times on each side, because he crawled well, and several times, I had picked Cody up and found the casts were left behind! He learned as an infant how to break plaster and remove cast padding. It did not take much of that before the casts would just slide off. The orthopedic doctor, his staff, and all of us began to realize very early the truth of the statement I already made. He was a monkey with a handicap. Still, even with all the recasting, it had worked. The clubfeet were corrected. Therefore, we believed the pavloc harness would correct his hips too. We just did not realize yet how complicated spina bifida is.

On the morning of our appointment, we arrived at 6:30 A.M., did hip x-rays, and waited to see the doctor. When he called us in, he put the x-rays on the view box and made this statement with lightening speed, "The harness did not work. Go to the hospital and pre-register for hip surgery next week. He will need both hips done, he will need two units of blood designated for him, and the surgery will last several hours. Sign the consents. I'll see you there."

With that, he turned and started to leave the room. I was so in shock. I cried out, "Whoa, whoa, whoa." He wheeled around with an astonished look on his face. I explained as calmly as I could, "Dr. D., this is my baby you are talking about. I don't really know if you are used to talking to apathetic parents or just those afraid to ask questions, but that is not enough information for me. I need to know what the benefits of the surgery are, how dangerous it is, what type of anesthesia he will require, and for how long, and what will happen if we don't do it."

He came back and sat down. He carefully answered all of my questions. I told him that I did not want to hurt his feelings in any way, but that we would want to get a second opinion. He said that was fine. I left crying that day and headed home armed with a copy of the films and very bad news. That night as I shared the news with our family (all of the people who had helped us to carefully put him in and out of that awful harness for the seven months since his birth), the mood was very grim. The only thing we knew to do was to make an appointment with a well-known specialist 100 miles to the west and hope he had a better plan. For two weeks I cried and prayed, and then we saw the second doctor. He looked at the films. (I had not brought any notes from our doctor so I could be sure nothing influenced his opinion.) He said almost word for word what Dr. D. had said. That was one of the few times we ever got a second opinion. Our doctors were excellent. In the end, it had just been an expensive way of padding our confidence in our own doctor. The surgery would need to be done. We headed home to try and brace ourselves to survive it. Doctors putting our infant to sleep, cutting on both of his tiny hips, and then putting him into a body cast for two months. Horror.

The surgery was scheduled for ten days after that appointment. I don't believe we slept at all those nine nights. One thing I did, which seemed so crazy to others but I felt strongly led to do, was take Cody to have his picture made. I'm not sure why that was so extremely important, but these are some of the thoughts that run through your mind, *If anything goes wrong, I want everyone to know how he looked before. I want to remember him as the precious little happy baby he is now. If he dies, at least we will have pictures made right before the surgery.* Not the thoughts, I know, that most mothers of babies ever go near. I longed to be one of those mothers. If I had known then that it would be the second of 15 surgeries he would have to endure, we could have taken the whole family to have our pictures made because none of us would have survived. That must be why God alone is allowed to know what's coming.

Cody's surgery was slated for 7 A.M. on a Monday morning. I wanted to stay home with Paul and Cody that weekend, but I knew I needed to work to enable me to be off longer after the surgery. I was thankful I had been in that job for nine years, had job security, and had supportive people to work with. Even then, I realized it would take a full effort on my part to maintain a career and raise this very challenging child.

Now I had worked the day before to get in as many hours as possible, and all day long, I had this stabbing pain behind my left ear. My glasses were new and I had the left temple padded like a cast. My supervisor, who was also my friend, told me, "You take those glasses back because I have never heard you whine so much since I have known you." She was right. I was not a whiner, but this was not a normal pain. I just worked on, thinking I would deal with it after the surgery.

Therefore, I rose the next morning at the usual 5 A.M. waking time and immediately realized something was wrong. I really thought I was just weary from the waiting and worrying. However, when I went into the bathroom and looked into the mirror, I was horrified to see the whole right side of my face drawn. I quickly checked to see if I had feeling in that arm, hand, leg, and foot, and was relieved to discover that I did. I panicked. *My Lord, I have had a stroke.* I then realized it was only facial paralysis. I thought, *My dad just left us. Paul's dad just died. His mom is very ill. My mom is a wreck. Cody has to have big hip surgery. I refuse to let anything else bad happen to us. I will get dressed and go to work. Paul worked until midnight, so I am not going to wake him up. I will be fine.* I started brushing my teeth and the water ran down my chin uncontrolled. *I don't care. It will work itself out.* My right eye was only halfway opened. I just felt I couldn't take on anything else. I felt so weak and frightened. *Lord, whatever this is, please show me how to make it go away.* I dressed and drove to work.

When I walked into the NICU for morning report, everyone gasped. My face must have looked worse than I let myself believe it did. I had kept shades on to try and hide the paralysis. When I removed them, I could see the horror on their faces. When they asked what was wrong, I replied, "Nothing, I just slept hard. Let's give report." My supervisor motioned for me to go into the nurses' station while the rest received report. Tears flowed from my left eye; my right eye wouldn't even produce tears. She poked my eyebrow with a pin, which was very painful. She tried to remember what brought paralysis without loss of feeling. I did not want to know.

I ran to the rest room and locked the door. They sent one of the nursing assistants, one of my favorite people in the world, around there to try to coax me out. K. pleaded, "Come on out, Baby. (She calls everyone "Baby.") We love you no matter how you look." I would have laughed if I could have.

I didn't really think I looked like the hunchback of Notre Dame. I must have though, because over the next few weeks several of the staff would call and say to me, "You need to come on back around people that love you." Obviously, they believed the drawn face and eye was going to be a permanent condition. Even without knowing what it was, I had no intention of that happening.

So I came out, and they sent me off to our family practice doctor. I went reluctantly. He did some tests and in his cool way said, "Well, Raina, you have a little condition called Bell's palsy. Your paralysis is now 85 percent, but it will go to 100 percent, it always does." I was amazed. The news got worse. "Every now and then, it becomes a permanent condition."

Even with trouble speaking due to the paralysis in that side of my tongue, I rose up on that one and told him, "Oh no, Buddy. I have a handicapped child to raise, and I need all of my faculties to do that successfully. Give me the option with the best cure rate."

He laughed, "There is only one and that is steroids. The quicker we start them the better chance you will have for a full recovery."

"Draw the shot up and let her rip tater chip."

He smiled and asked, "Don't you want to know the dangers of steroids?"

I said, "I already do. How soon before this mess will clear up?"

"At least six weeks." His words shocked me. Six weeks! I needed it to be gone before Cody's surgery on Monday. I felt sick, but I knew what I had to do. The nurse gave me the shot, and I left with a completely new set of appointments to add to my already overloaded life.

When I arrived home, Paul met me on the front porch. He knew for me to be coming home at 10 A.M. something had to be askew. "What's wrong?" he asked. He looked frightened when he noticed my drawn face.

We were past trying to cushion bad news much, so I just said it. "I have Bell's palsy." Then I told him the details.

"Has anyone ever had it on both sides?"

"Well, Paul, I guess I will be the world's first case."

We laugh about it now, but it was far from funny then. We went inside, sat in the den, and just stared into space for a long time. Finally, he said, "It's okay, Baby. The medicine will cure it in a few weeks. Go lie down and rest. You know I love you no matter what. We just have too much on us. I thought you had suffered a stroke. At least it isn't that. Unplug the phone in the bedroom. I will handle the calls and the baby in here."

I just blubbered, "I love you" and followed his instructions. When I went into the bathroom, I saw how really awful my face looked. I put two false tears (eye drops) into my right eye, laid down, and fell asleep praying, *"Help me, Lord."* I was totally exhausted.

I awoke a couple of hours later to a lot of chatter. I had new resolve. I began to call our lives the Job syndrome. I thought, *Whatever God has for me to face, I will, and I won't let my faith waiver.* That would be huge.

When I opened the bedroom door, several members of our family were there. They gasped when they saw me and began to cry. Cody reached for me smiling and mouthed, "Momma." Bell's palsy had not kept him from recognizing his mom.

I told everyone else this, "Before you ask, I am not going to move the date of his surgery. The dread is too agonizing. This will last at least six weeks. I just need someone to go and buy me some very long straws so I can get liquids past the paralysis. Otherwise, it is onward as planned."

They all said in unison, "Are you sure?"

I answered emphatically, "Very. I don't want any more waiting. Otherwise, I might have a stroke too." They were bewildered. What I learned from that experience was that if you get under too much stress, your body would react in some way—hives, Bell's palsy, or maybe even a stroke or a heart attack. I was thankful that it was something I could recover from. I felt that if we all lived past Cody's hip surgery, I would recover in time.

Everyone had talked of all of the negatives of Bell's palsy to me, but no one had shared the benefits of being on steroids. I hated the palsy, the dry, droopy eye, chewing my tongue up because of the paralysis, etc., but good always comes out of bad and several benefits came from it. I had more offers of help than ever before. I'm sure it was pity, which I usually hate, but in that case, I welcomed any port in the storm. Between worrying and not being able to eat solid food, I lost weight. Mainly, that medicine made me feel like I could leap tall buildings with a single bound. Oddly enough, the staring I endured helped me over the next few years to be empathetic to the staring Cody had to endure and learn how to deal with.

We arrived at the local Catholic hospital at 5 A.M. on Monday morning for the hip surgery. The whole family and many friends and church members were there, frightened, but with faith that God would watch over Cody and see us through. Paul had given two units of blood so we would not have to worry, thank God, about the risk of undesignated blood. I will never forget how tiny Cody looked on that big stretcher with that hospital gown and paper cap on. The most difficult by far was when they pinned a little Saint Christopher medallion on his armband and carried him beyond those double doors to surgery. I wanted to be in another universe. I don't really recall who was there or what they said. I knew Paul and our moms and our sisters were crying and were afraid for Cody and for me. The only thing I could slur out was, "If he is okay, I'll be okay." It was true. The rest of the time I spent praying.

That two-and-a-half-hour surgery seemed like it took days to complete. My imagination ran wild. All the sweet people in my family and our friends took turns trying to comfort me. I love them, but it was like bees buzzing in my ear. I looked awful—sleep deprived and scared and ol' Bell's palsy to boot. Needless to say, I did not win the "queen of the surgery waiting room" award that day. There was another angel there, a little lady they have assigned to go to the surgery door, check on the patient, and report back to the family. Paul and I wore her out during that surgery. In fact, the last time we sent her in to check on him she returned with this message, "Dr. D. says he is closing now and not to send me in there again." Others laughed; I made no promises.

One of the things we learned that day, which held true all of the next 13 times we would be required to spend restless hours in a surgery waiting area, is that every day of our lives there are people suffering, and unless you are there, you tune it out. Family after family had to endure bad news that day. Surgery had revealed cancer, improper functioning kidneys, on and on. The most outstanding memory was a young wife talking and laughing one minute, feeling confident that her 39-year-old husband would be fine and around to help her raise three children under ten years old. The next minute she was screaming and crying with news of terminal lung cancer and a prognosis of 3 to 6 months of life left. You never forget things like that. I had looked at pictures of the three children. After the doctor's report, I wished I had not. I wanted out of there before the Bell's palsy did become permanent.

Finally, Dr. D. emerged smiling and declared, "Calm down. Cody is fine. A couple of things caused the delays. First off, they told you the wrong blood type. He is your type instead of Paul's blood type. I decided to wait to tell you if we needed to give blood, which we didn't. Secondly, his IV came out right after we slept him. We called in a surgeon, but the cut-down he tried to do in his neck was unsuccessful. We made it through the surgery with a 23-gauge butterfly needle in his scalp. When he wakes up, we will send him to PICU overnight, then if he is doing well, on to the floor in the morning. Are there any questions?" I was overwhelmed. *What was the purpose of the little report lady if she did not give an accurate report? We had been told everything was going fine while they were struggling with wrong blood types and infiltrated IV's.* If he could have understood me, I would have thrown a fit.

After years more experience, I say this, "A child in the hospital without an advocate is in danger. However, very little in life goes along with perfect plans." Cody could have taken Paul's blood. It would not have been ideal, but he could have. The IV situation was handled the same way I would have handled it. There were better surgeons in town to try cut-downs, but they were not available and Dr. D.'s team was watching very carefully. They knew what a state I was in, and they wanted to keep me from worrying more.

You have to pick your battles. You have to pick a health-care team you trust, and let them do their job. Otherwise, you are always on a rampage and you will burn out early with a defect like spina bifida. Keep a very watchful eye; throw a fit if you need to, but only if you need to. Remember, you will need to be healthy to help your child through all the medical challenges. Stress and high blood pressure can take that health away. There are always horror stories. If your team's name is attached to an unusual number of them, pick a different team. Otherwise, keep watch, keep calm, and let them know what you expect. With a child who will require so many surgeries, you are lost without trust. We trusted God and our team.

Very little has been perfect, but Cody is thriving. He still has some physical issues. He always will. After all, his spine and all those nerves suffered damage before birth. No one can undo that. Mentally, he is very sound. Part of that stems from the love and care his doctors and nurses have given him. They are an extension of family in our hearts. I made a mental note that day, and after that, we were given more details. It worked out.

Well, praise the Lord, Cody had his hips fixed! Our recall later would be, "That was the first time he had his hips fixed." I decided I would go to the cafeteria and eat something liquid, because it was going to be a long night on the other side of the PICU door.

Before the elevator came, a recovery room nurse came to find me and report, "Ms. Raina, they are taking Cody to his room."

"What!" I demanded. "What happened to overnight in PICU?"

The nurse's reply was, "Honey, he woke up in that big spica cast and was trying to jump off the stretcher, so we are taking him straight to the room."

My exclamation was, "That's my boy! Forget lunch, I'm headed to the room!"

"They will bring you lunch anyway," she explained. Apparently she had not noticed the palsy, and I did not want to draw attention to it, but I thought, *Unless it is all liquids, I won't be eating it.*

I was so excited rushing back to the room. My baby had his hips in place permanently, and he hadn't even needed blood. We would come to accept shortly that no matter how many surgeries a child has, they don't come with warranties, and the only thing permanent about a disability was being disabled. The best advice we ever got and the smartest thing we ever did was to learn to let attitude be the driving force in Cody's life instead of repair work.

None of us were prepared for what we saw when we entered that room. Our baby was as pale as the sheet. The "trying to jump off the stretcher" statement the recovery room nurse made had fooled us into thinking he would look like he had that morning going in. Not even close. You see, most people judge according to what they are used to. Most patients in recovery are either out of it or throwing up. So by their standards, Cody was doing excellently. By ours, being our child, his appearance was frightening. His eyes were weak, he had a cast from his armpits to his toes, the only cut out was to cram a diaper in, and a solid plaster bar spread his legs about two feet apart. He had bruises from IV attempts and three stitches and swelling in his neck from the attempted cut-down. The working IV was in the middle of his forehead, and one look was all it took for us to know our little baby had been through a heck of an ordeal. I was glad he was sleeping, because I believe at that moment the impact of the surgery and the impact of Bell's palsy collided, and I sank to the floor—exhausted, frightened, and depressed. "God help us!" I cried out. Poor Paul, I scared him to death. He helped me up enough to sit on the cot they had put in the room for me to sleep on. I was sobbing. None of my friends with infants less than a year old could even imagine putting their babies through such a thing. I wanted to take him home. I wanted to see him smile. Hard times.

We lived through that day and ten more days in the hospital with IV's. A stack of notes came daily from prayer-chain participants in several churches and Mom's Eastern Star group. They were such welcome and comforting reading. A note came that his picture had been placed in the prayer room at First West. It is still there. It is like a piece of wallpaper in there. Through all the crises of Cody's life, prayer chains have helped. They are citywide, including McGuire Methodist where I grew up going to church. What a blessing knowing Christian people, even strangers, were lifting up prayers for our son.

The steroid high helped too, because Cody and I stayed up most of those nights in misery. That cast was shaped where it did not fit anywhere well. I held him on a pillow in my lap through each night, and we rocked and we sang and we watched TV Land. I memorized the all night sequence: *Andy Griffith, I Love Lucy, Leave It To Beaver,* etc. Of course, I wouldn't let anyone stay but me. I just kept thinking of how much having his hips in the sockets would help him. Well, we survived to be discharged home. When we got home, we worked out ways to prop the cast up in a sitting position, and we discovered the wonderful world of *Winnie the Pooh* on video. Every crisis brought a new rescuer. Those tapes were it for that one. There was a series of four then, and we watched them so much that Paul and I memorized every word.

During the six weeks following the surgery in the spica, two strange things happened. One was funny, the other horrible. First, I kept telling Paul that the TV had a short in it because it changed channels by itself. He said, "That's crazy. A short would not make it change channels and it has no self. It's a piece of equipment."

I scoffed, "Thanks, Mr. Smarty. You are a lot of help." Of course, it would not happen when he was watching. The other thing was the remote was often missing. I had other people to check the TV and nothing could be found malfunctioning. Finally, one day Paul was there, and the channel did change without our help. At the same time, we saw Cody flash something and heard him giggle. Then we learned the secret of the auto-changing channels. The little monkey had removed cast padding enough to hide the "mote" in the front of the cast and had been changing channels when we weren't looking and putting the remote back in its hiding place. What a child!

The other occurrence is a scary memory. Ma, Cody's beloved grandmother, is a great cook. One of her main contributions to our recovery was to keep meals coming. On this Saturday when we were both home, she had made homemade chicken and dumplings and brought lunch to us. Of course, I couldn't eat any because Ms. Bell's Palsy was still visiting me, but Paul and Cody could. By trial and error, we had learned how to keep the cast clean, how to give a good sponge bath around a body cast, and how to prop him in the high chair to eat. I cut up small bites of chicken and dumplings and put them on the high chair tray. Cody was eating with his baby spoon, and somehow he got choked—that turning blue, air-hunger choked. I knew as a Basic Life Support instructor to give back blows and chest thrusts, but the cast was too high up for any of that. I demanded of Paul, "Go get the hammer, and we will tear the cast off. We can always recast him." Paul didn't move. I looked at him and the best description I can give of his color is silver. I cried out, "Lord, help me. I have a blue, choked baby and a silver husband." I did the only thing I knew to do, something I had been trained and had trained others not to do, a finger sweep. On that occasion, it was the only choice and it worked. The dumpling pieces dislodged, and Cody took a gasp, then he began to cry. What a welcome scream. I put him in my lap, and we rocked away the fear.

After Cody was calm and breathing well, Paul reported in a winded voice, "My chest is hurting. I need you to take me to the emergency room."

He was alarmed when my comeback was, "Sorry, Pal. I can only handle one near-death experience in our three-person family per day. I will call an ambulance for you." He had huge drops of sweat on his forehead. He got a cool cloth and lay down with it on his forehead. After a few minutes, with the full assurance that Cody was okay, the chest pain subsided. Right after that, Ma came in. Upon hearing the story, she developed a huge white ring around her mouth, which was always her reaction to fear. I slurred out to her and Paul, "Useless. All this time I have been going to work thinking my baby would be safe if an emergency arose. I see right now, y'all are useless." We all laughed and the mood lightened. They will neither one serve Cody dumplings (even at age 17), unless I am near. Some things you never forget. Cody choking and turning blue was one of them.

Six weeks to the day, the Bell's palsy started to clear up, and I made an almost complete recovery. I hoped Ms. Bell would never visit again, and so far, she hasn't.

Eight weeks after the surgery, we went to Dr. D.'s office to face the cast cutter. That thing was scary as it moved over that big cast—up and down the inside and outside of the legs, all the way to his tiny toes. That was the first time I came to appreciate the skill of the cast guy in that doctor's office. He and Cody later became buddies and even shared stories about wrestling.

Cody was delighted to be reunited with the big bathtub and long-splashing bubble baths. We learned how to help scars heal. The nurse in Dr. D.'s office helped us so much then and was so kind, just as is the nurse there now. The employees of all the local physical therapy departments were beginning to form lifelong friendships with Cody and with us. Cody was on target with all growth and development up to fifteen months except, of course, he still could not walk. At that point, I looked Dr. D. in the eye and I delivered this statement, "Whatever it takes, however difficult or time consuming, we want to do what it takes for him to walk." He has been such a wonderful doctor and person and has always had such a neat way of following and promoting Cody's progress. He agreed and wrote orders.

The first appliance was called a parapodium. It consisted of a solid, wooden platform with a full set of braces mounted to it. When Cody was strapped in it, he looked like a spaceman, but it was so good to see him standing up straight. One of the things I miss most to this day is his standing up and giving me a hug. Oh well, I just had to learn to stoop to the level of the wheelchair. Just a little inconvenience. If your kids can walk into a room and hug you, don't ever take that for granted.

The first time we went to physical therapy, I was so excited for him to learn how to walk in the parapodium. It didn't matter that we had to drive to a hospital fifteen miles away in mostly bumper-to-bumper traffic. My boy was going to walk, and this was the first stage to getting there. I would gladly have driven 150 miles each way. Right away Cody started charming the employees and making new friends, starting on our first visit with the people in admissions. When we arrived in the PT department, I discovered that the charge PT was a lady I knew from the hospital where I worked. She was in charge of our PT department for many years until they opened this new facility. It really is a good thing to be kind and treat everyone in your path the way you want to be treated, because you never know where life will take you. Sometimes people get an opportunity to return a kindness or whatever treatment they received from you. I say be kind.

The first thing Ms. G. did was sit me down, look me in the eye, and tell me emphatically that I would need to be very patient. She explained, "It will take him at least one year to learn to walk in the parapodium." She went on to explain that most spina bifida kids were three years old before they could handle it, and he was only fifteen months old. She added a lot of physical therapy talk about swinging gait, etc. I was, to say the least, stunned. A whole year. Wow! Just to learn one little piece of equipment. It was another depressing moment, but only for a moment.

For all of my life, I will remember what happened next. She stood Cody in that contraption and put a little walker with wheels on the front legs in front of him. She knelt down beside him and said this, "Cody, all I want you to do is to try to take a couple of steps. The way you do that is to swing your hips and sort of roll the platform under your feet while holding on to the handles of the walker in front of you. Do it really slowly, because if you lean too far forward you will fall. And because the braces do not bend, you will not be able to break your fall, and you will get hurt, okay?" Cody said nothing. I thought she had scared him. She repeated, "Okay? Do you understand what I told you? I will be right here to help you."

His only word was, "Okay." The PT room was about fifty feet

long. She moved, and before either one of us could say anything, Cody took off like a racehorse out of the stall, rolling that platform and pushing behind that tiny little walker. He did not slow down until he was at the end of the fifty feet. Both of us were amazed to the point of being speechless. The funny thing was Cody stood there with his back to us, and he didn't say anything. We took turns asking if he was okay, and then we quickly moved to that end of the room so we could see his face and found him standing there sleeping.

It was so amusing, and we said in unison, "I guess he's tired."

I picked the whole appliance up with him in it, and I gave him this praise. "Baby, you did so well. Are you okay?"

He responded, "I'm tired. Wet's go."(That's "Let's go." in toddler talk.)

Ms. G. was still in shock. After a few minutes, she called her assistant. When she arrived, Ms. G. related to her what had happened, and they both laughed. She asked of the other lady, "I don't know any fifteen-month-olds in reciprocating braces, do you?" That was the next appliance to use in walking training.

The other lady replied, "Never heard of it."

I interrupted them with, "Just because it hasn't been done before doesn't mean it can't be done now."

Shocked, they looked at each other, and Ms. G. reported, "Well, I guess I will go call Dr. D., but I don't know if they can make cables that small."

I said, "Tell him I said to think outside the box. It's called creativity." She laughed and I smiled, but I was serious.

It would become typical for Cody. He was extraordinary. I had already realized that, but I wondered in that moment how many handicapped individuals just need an advocate, a strong-willed person. Someone to say, "So what? Let's try it anyway. You miss 100 percent of the shots you never take." As the years went by, we discovered the answer. Many, many, many people and not just disabled ones need an advocate. Of course, toddlers always need someone to speak up for them. Unfortunately, the world is also full of those who don't have enough courage to face adversity with a positive attitude. I hope sharing Cody's story helps some people to understand that. This was absolutely not the only time we butted up against resistance and then scaled the wall.

At that point, we began a long and challenging journey for all of us: Cody, the family, PT, Dr. D., the brace people, Special Children's Services, and our team, our mostly wonderful team. The husband of one of the therapists was a very quiet man, and he got her to ask me if he could build Cody some parallel bars from painted wood and PVC pipes. I was thrilled, and he even built PVC extensions that we could raise to make them higher when necessary. We were able to use them for several years. One of my favorite pictures of Cody is at age 2 in a navy short set with a red bucket hat on, walking on those bars. It is our "first steps" photo. So when our friends had beautiful coffee tables in their living rooms, we had parallel bars, and we were glad. Nobody expects a construction worker to be an angel, but it happens.

Before we were done, we would travel to PT there twice a week for five years, and Cody would wind up charming people in every department on the first floor of that facility, plus some outside agency people. One very hot July day when Cody was 2, we journeyed out to PT. On arriving at the front door of the hospital Cody was greeted by the head of the ladies' auxiliary with a huge bouquet of balloons, silver balloons, and the largest one read, "He's here!" which is, of course, for a newborn boy. The lady gave him a big hug and kiss, then turned to me and reported, "Cody is our favorite customer of all time in the gift shop. We just love him and he is the cutest thing we ever saw."

I smiled and told her, "Thank you," and we moved on. Cody was moving well by now at the age of 2, in those reciprocating braces they hadn't known if they could make that small, with a walker in front of him. He was a charmer. The next stop was admissions where his friend Linda worked. The silly, nonfriendly system of having to go to admissions on every visit and get a new account number and stamper card had been implemented by then. During Cody's five years of PT, he received 520 account numbers. How crazy is that? God help us! He did. Although financially the whole thing has been, and still is, outrageous, I refuse to write much about that. Suffice it to say that God kept us afloat. He provided what we needed when we needed it. He still does.

Cody went in singing, "Help me, Linda. Help, help me, Linda." That lady smiled from ear to ear along with the rest of the employees and patients there. Some even clapped. I had long since stopped being embarrassed by his performances, and I surely did not have the heart to tell him that the song actually says, "Help me, Rhonda."

With stamper card in hand, we moved on to PT. He had a grand reception there, too, and on the toddler-sized bench where he usually sat and rested, there was a variety of four each of chips and sodas and a large hatbox. I asked, "What is all of that?" At this point, he was so loved there I felt like an intruder. (Like if he could only drive at 2, I could have stayed home!)

Ms. G. declared, "Well, I want you to know you have the most socially precocious child I have ever met." (My face flushed at that.) "The chip and coke guys brought all these and said Cody doesn't like the same snacks each time so they brought him a choice." By then Cody had opened the hatbox and had put this huge, wide-brimmed, very expensive western hat on his head. He could hardly see out from under it. She went on, "The hat is a gift from Billy in Biomed. He said that Cody passes him in the hall every time he is walking, and he always remarks, 'Hi, Cowboy! I like your hat.' So he had to go to the western store and buy him one just like it." Later on I met Cowboy Billy, and the man was so shy he could hardly talk to me. Cody's ability to make friends was, and is, amazing.

Well, I left Cody there, as usual, because all involved said children work better if the parents were not there. I trusted that, so I went to the front lobby and sat for the hour. When I returned, Cody was standing in the same spot where I left him. On the floor at the 50-foot away end, were candy bars. I asked, "What's going on?"

Ms. G. snapped, "Nothing, exactly nothing."

I replied, "What do you mean?"

She said in an exasperated tone, "Another thing about Cody is his strong will." My face flushed for the second time in one session. She continued, "If he wants to he will walk from here to the next town, and if he doesn't, he will make a hole in this floor before he will move one inch. Those candy bars are bribes that did not work. We have been in this same spot for one hour. Thank goodness that does not happen often." (I was in total agreement since the therapy cost was $100 per hour.)

I felt like she wanted me to fuss at him, but I didn't. He was 2, and she was the one who had let me know we were asking difficult things of him at an extremely early age. I pushed when I felt it was necessary, but if he went into shutdown every now and then even as a toddler, I wasn't going to challenge his judgment. My only instructions were, "Let's go."

As unhappy as Cody was with her report, he had something to share with me first. Lying on the hyperbaric chamber table in the back room of PT, with her leg in the chamber, was a very large African-American lady. Cody commanded, "Come meet B. . . . She is my friend and she has a big ol' sore on her leg."

B. laughed, but I wondered how many embarrassing moments you could have in one PT session. That sweet lady said, "It's okay, Honey. Cody and I are good friends."

My response was, "It's a good thing."

She stated, "He is one precious child."

I told her, "Thanks and it was nice meeting you." At that moment, I wanted to take our balloons, chips, sodas, cowboy hat, braces, walker, and "precious child" and get out of there. So I did. However, the session was not quite over. When we hit the outside door and the extreme heat, I explained to Cody, "I'm going to stand you here in the shade of this little tree and go get the car."

As I reached the end of the first row of cars, with all of his bundles plus my purse and a pair of arm crutches we were working with, while sweating profusely and about to collapse, Cody screamed from his shady spot, "Hurry up, you cazy Momma, or I'm gonna break a sweat."

I yelled back, "On my way, Son. We can't have that."

Paul's grandmother summed it up perfectly years later, when she was 82 as I was helping her up one day. She said, "I know, you are doing all the work, and I am doing all of the blowing."

When I got Cody buckled in the car seat that day and we started home, I asked him, "Son, what did they tell you in therapy today?" I just wanted to know if they fussed at him.

His reply was, "Oh, you know, Momma. The same thing they always say in terapy. (That's "therapy" in toddler talk.) 'Shut your mouth and move your butt, and shut your mouth and move your butt,' but I didn't do it, not today."

I just said, "Well, all righty then. You were all over that, Buddy." Thank the Lord all five hundred and twenty sessions were not like that one. The strong will would become a blessing later. All I know is, his legs have never really worked right, but he taught all of us how to walk right over the top of the challenges in our lives.

He *was* a socially precocious child. We spent many hours in the waiting rooms of doctor's offices, and he began to work the room on each of those occasions. Once we were in the urologist's office waiting room, and Cody was restless that day. He was not quite 2, but when a child has a deficit caused by a birth defect, the body compensates or enables him to compensate, by making the other senses or abilities stronger. Cody's greatest ability was speech. He came from a long line of talkers, and you could tell it. He would ask each person waiting how old they were, how many times they had been there, and if they had ever received a shot from that doctor's nurse. Vital information to him. As time went on, I had to convince him not to ask ladies how old they were to avoid offending and embarrassing them. I also let him know that if he kept inviting strangers home for supper he would have to learn how to cook, which, of course, has not happened yet.

On this occasion, he was visiting around the waiting area while I read, and he came from across the room and said, "Mom, this is Joe." I looked up to see a white-headed man probably in his 70s.

I sheepishly replied, "Hi, Joe."

Cody continued, "Back when Joe was young he went to school at Duke University and played basketball for them. He got a college degree there and became an engineer. He is retired now and has kidney trouble. That's why he comes here, but he hasn't ever had a shot. I told him he should come over and visit and eat with us sometimes. He said he might."

I said, "That's great. Maybe he can." I don't think the old guy or I either one could have been more embarrassed. It was a typical scenario created by my son. Joe must have played on one of the first basketball teams Duke ever had.

Because we had so many appointments, we avoided Fridays because of my work schedule and Mondays because I was exhausted from 40-hour weekends at work. That scheduling resulted in our visiting the neurosurgeon the morning of his second birthday. At the end of the visit, I needed to make a follow-up appointment. I sent Cody just on the other side of the door to wait with the patients who had not been seen yet, while I made the appointment and paid. Five minutes later he pushed through the door waving a hand full of money. He exclaimed, "Mom, look what I got."

My alarmed response was, "Where in the world did you get all of that money?"

His answer was, "Well, I just happened to mention that it was my birthday and some little ladies in the waiting room pulled out a bunch of money and gave it to me. Cool, huh?"

I said, "No, it is not cool and you march right back out there and give it back. You can not take up a collection from people waiting to see the doctor, Son." He was stupefied by my response.

He countered with, "But Mom, they really, really, really wanted me to have it. They said I was so cute." I took Mr. Cute and left by the back door that day. Dr. J.'s staff had a good laugh at Cody and me both.

We went home that day and had a big blowout birthday party with kids, balloons, and swimming. Paul dressed up like Batman and swung into the party on a rope. Paul's family was there, including Cody's first cousin Jamie. They are very close. We all had a blast. The child got enough money and gifts to fill a room. That evening when everyone else in the family, including Cody, was exhausted and sleeping, I cried as I cleaned up the mess from the party.

My dad, now remarried for about a year, had not come, called, or sent Cody anything. His only grandchild; I could not understand it. We had been very close when I was growing up, until I was 31 and needed my support systems to help me to survive the hardship of enduring what spina bifida is. I was so very angry with him and made a promise to myself to let him know it the next time I talked to him. There was no next time. The very next night at midnight, the state police came and told us that he and his wife had both been killed in an automobile accident.

The first thing I thought about was my anger and the saying I was taught as a child that I often reiterate to my children, *Be careful, little mouth, what you say.* I thanked God that "next time" had not come and afforded me the chance to express my anger over the forgotten birthday. He was gone. "The fat lady had sung." In an instant, our lives were changed again. I cried out for God's help and He sent earthly angels to help us. Sadness and joy were entwined so tightly in the life of that child. As before, I relied on prayer to survive. God always showed up.

At 2, Cody was becoming one of the cutest and most personable toddlers ever. He would do things like sit in the tub at night and look at his potbelly and say, "I need to weduce. ("Reduce" in toddler talk.) I really need to weduce." I would try to comfort him by telling him he was thin and all toddler boys have potbellies.

During one such conversation I told him, "Baby, it's okay. You usually eat things at lunch like a turkey sandwich. That's not fattening."

He said, "Not until daddy slaps that mayonnaise to it." His speech and intelligence and reasoning were amazing.

The final memorable episode at Special Children's Services happened on a very dismal day. We started out very early, as always, and held hands on our way there in the dark. (He and I always held hands in the car. It made us both feel better. Later on, I would have to explain that people might talk about us if we didn't break that habit. However, it set a good example for him to learn to drive one handed, which is required when driving with hand controls.)

As we neared the clinic that morning, the dark clouds rolled in. It was frightening, but all the children and caretakers were there as scheduled, so we signed in and took a spot in the front waiting area. All of a sudden the electricity went off, both glass front doors swung open, and golf ball-sized hail came down by the tons. Cody started screaming, "It's a winter storm! Hit the deck! It's a winter storm! Hit the deck!" He dove to the floor and the other children were screaming, crying, and diving to the floor as I tried to clamp my hand over his mouth. What a mess! It only lasted a few minutes, but his verbal alarms never stopped, no matter what I said. The only injuries were to cars in the parking lot, the roof, and children's bruises from diving under the chairs. In a conversation about it later, the social workers were laughing and asking me why he reacted that way. All I could say was, "I have no idea. He has never seen a winter storm in his life. Nobody I know has winter storms in May." That child was a mess.

Hail and all, they had clinic that day. It was just too hard to keep rescheduling everything. Even without the hail damage to our cars, it would have been an awful, unbelievable day because Dr. D. unloaded the news that his hips were out of socket again. They would have to be redone—one at a time—and this time they would put surgical steel pins in, which would have to be surgically removed six months after insertion. They were kin to huge metal screws. At some point, he wanted to move muscles from Cody's butt to his thighs because the muscles that let you sit Indian-style did not work. A hailstorm and plans for five more surgeries were almost more than we could handle, but we did. In and out of the hospital for months, spica casts, IV meds, pain . . . what a nightmare—more surgery waiting room time than I wanted to think about. During those times, plastic football heroes took the place of "Winnie the Pooh" as our rescuer. Many times in the hospital, we set up opposing teams on his over-the-bed table and played some championship games.

When we thought we were about to see light at the end of the tunnel, three of the most horrid events to date happened. After the removal of the last spica, surviving the chainsaw-sounding cast cutter, etc., we took Cody home to rush to the bathtub, as usual, because two months of sponge bathing is tough. As I was helping him into the tub, I noticed an open wound the size of a dime on his right buttocks. It already looked infected, so I immediately returned to Dr. D.'s office. They were not impressed. They told me just to put a TELFA pad on it to keep it dry. I didn't feel comfortable about it, so I went and talked to the pharmacist. He told me to put antibiotic cream on it. None of them seemed alarmed so I followed their suggestions. It was one of those times when I mistakenly ignored my gut instinct and followed the advice of others. The result was life threatening for Cody.

Three days later my aunt was in town. Ma, Cheryl, my aunt, and I all thought it would be fun to go to the mall, and we all believed Cody needed to go on an outing. He was unusually restless and did not seem to be bouncing back as well as he had after other surgeries. We had been at the mall for about an hour when Cody began to act strangely. He was talking about climbing mountains with Ma, and he was fake laughing. I felt of his head and it almost burned my hand. To top that off, not only was everyone scattered in different directions but also a heavy rainstorm had arrived. I found Ma first and asked her to find my aunt and sister because we needed to go to the hospital emergency room—then Cody and I went to wait in the car. *Oh, God, what in the world made us come to the mall? Why didn't I keep pressing about that wound until someone treated it? Please, God, help us get to the ER in time to help him. I was so stupid.* Parents always carry guilt. I'm not sure what my bad decision had been, but I knew I had made one, even though I was so meticulous with his care, both in and out of casts.

It took Ma a while to gather them up, and Cody was purple, hot as a firecracker, and talking crazy as we sped through the storm to the emergency room. When we arrived, I jumped out of the car and ran in, demanding immediate help. I was not about to deal with registration, forms, or any delay of any type in seeing the doctor. Only another child who was not breathing could have beaten us to medical care on that Sunday afternoon. There was no other child that ill, and the nurses took one look at Cody and jumped into action. When checked, his temperature registered at 106.4 degrees. They rechecked it three times. My heart was pounding. The nurse asked, "Would you mind stepping out while we do an assessment?"

I replied, "I will be leaning on the door. Get Dr. R., our pediatrician right now, please." I suppose they had already paged him because two minutes later he appeared. He asked why I wasn't in there with Cody, and when I related their request for me to go out, he was furious and took me in with him. Cody was packed in ice, he was purple, and he was extremely frightened. They were drawing blood and Dr. R. explained to them that I ran a NICU, and I could handle blood drawing. He was right, and I appreciated his coming to my defense. I could even have drawn the blood myself, but watching my child in that situation was almost unbearable.

They moved him quickly to the pediatric floor for the experienced nurses to start his IV. When we arrived, the nurse was someone I had worked with in that facility years before. I thought, *Thank God, an old friend. We could use a friend about now.* Her only question was, "Do you mind if I take him to the treatment room and try to start his IV?" What was it with the separation thing? I was scared to death and so was Cody. We didn't need to be separated. However, it was not time for a disagreement.

So I told her, "All I want is the IV in and the antibiotics started as quickly as possible please." I felt like saying, "I don't care if you take him on the rooftop, just hurry." I knew it was tension causing me to be upset with her, so I said nothing else.

She took him across the hall to the treatment room. I called Paul. There were no cell phones then so that was the first chance I had to call. He panicked, hung up the phone, and appeared before the IV and meds were infusing. A few moments later, the nurse reappeared with Cody. The IV and meds were going. She reported, "Honey, that is one smart kid. As sick as he is, he told me what vein to put it in, how to tape it, and everything."

I replied, "Well, he has been through a lot and has that IV thing down pat." Cody's temperature curved up and down for several days, and he slept a lot. We were terrified, but at the end of ten days, he was free of fever, the wound was closed, and we went home, exhausted. I remember walking around the yard and sobbing, suffering from that horrible crash-and-burn you go through after critical episodes like that, thinking it was too much. It was one of the most depressing times since his birth. Shortly, our situation was to become even more depressing, as unimaginable as that was.

Two weeks after his being discharged, I got out the walker and began a home therapy session. I stood Cody behind it and instructed him to walk. He took one step and fell to his knees. I gently stood him up again and begged him to take a few more steps. He couldn't. He started wailing and Paul picked him up and yelled at me, "Can't you see it hurts when he walks? Leave him alone and give him time to heal! You push too hard!"

I ran out of the house, over to Ma's house next door, where nobody was home, sat in a rocking chair on her patio, and sobbed. That was a most horrible moment. I had allowed all those surgeries, pins in, pins out, moving muscles, body casts, fever so high it was a miracle he had not had a febrile seizure, and I wanted to see results. I wanted to find some benefit from all of that pain my child had suffered. I will never forget and I will always regret that day. It took a lot of prayer, apologizing to both Paul and Cody, and a large batch of chocolate brownies for us to go forward.

During that period, I began to get calls from spina bifida kids' parents who needed guidance. Some would even call me from the surgery waiting room, crying and asking for help. I began to realize there were many suffering like us who had less help, less faith, and weaker family ties. My mind began to reach for ideas of how I could help more.

During that same period, we received some news that really threw us a curve. I was pregnant. We were in shock. Before we could adjust, I began to bleed. At twelve weeks of pregnancy, I was instructed by my doctor to stay in bed for the entire weekend. I did that, and on Monday morning the bleeding was worse. I was sent for an ultrasound and an exam; a miscarriage had occurred. Dr. H.'s nurse was there, the same precious nurse friend who had been so encouraging before Cody was born. She sat and cried with me, and then I was sent to the hospital. God has many angels on earth, but some are special. She qualifies, God love her. We didn't know how we exactly felt about having another baby so soon, but losing it was truly devastating.

One night a short time later, we got a call from a nursing super-visor telling us that Paul's mother was dying. We quickly dressed, took Cody next door to stay with Ma, and rushed to the hospital. She passed away that night. It was the greatest hurt I had seen Paul go through. We had lost three of our four parents and a baby in less than two years.

Around the same time, someone suggested we send Cody to a day care called Preschool Enrichment Program or PEP. I was hesitant, but for some reason at my mother-in-law's funeral, watching Paul in so much pain, I knew our lives needed some changes. Things were too intense. Paul and I were both barely moving from day-to-day. I thought of a saying I had learned years before:

> *When you are blue,*
> *Find something to do,*
> *For someone who is sadder than you.*[11]

We needed change. Maybe day care would help Cody. Maybe I could write a book to help other families. It wouldn't bring our parents back, it wouldn't bring the baby we lost back, but if we put our hearts into it, it might bring us back.

I took Cody for an evaluation, suggested by Dr. J., in the same building where PEP was. The first thing I saw was some toddlers sign-ing. When I asked, they told me the day care had both handicapped and normal children. The toddlers had been signing to a deaf three year old.

Cody stayed in the evaluation for two hours. When I went in to get him, I was given this report, "Well, he won't need speech. We tested him through six years old with no misses, and we were afraid to go further. He won't need cognitive, nor occupational therapy, but we do think you should get him his own TV show."

I responded, "Let's go." They laughed.

However, when I took the report to Dr. J. in the hope of snuffing out the "will be severely retarded" prognosis that I hated so much, he only had this to say, "That's just a test they do."

I asked, "Is it like the chickenpox? Do you just wake up one morning and you are retarded?"

He threw chart papers and exclaimed, "Momma, you wear me out!"

"Ditto."

He demanded, "What did you say?"

I said it again, "Ditto. You wear me out too. Everyone else says he is brilliant, and you say 'severely retarded.' There is a long distance between the two." He explained the hydrocephalus again, and we left. I know he had to err on the side of caution and prepare us for the worst, but that was rough.

My husband brought me back to reality that day. In the car, as I was crying and relating to him the news, he asked, "Did he tell you Cody could get in a car wreck between now and the time he is 40?"

I demanded, "What does that mean?"

His revelation was, "Well, he went over everything else, so I just wondered if he covered that. Raina, no one but God can really know what will happen in the future or how smart Cody will be. We just don't get privileges to the details of his future. Dr. J. is only relating to you what could happen. Let's just take it as it comes and try to give him the best life we can."

You never know who will be the one to bail you out, to drop the ladder of hope down into the deep well of depression so you can climb up—maybe not to the mountaintop, but at least to level ground—at least up to where there is light and air.

We needed help. We needed change. We felt Cody would benefit from being around other children, and we were anxious to see how other experts viewed his abilities. I would sign him up and start taking him to PEP right away. Writing the book would take years.

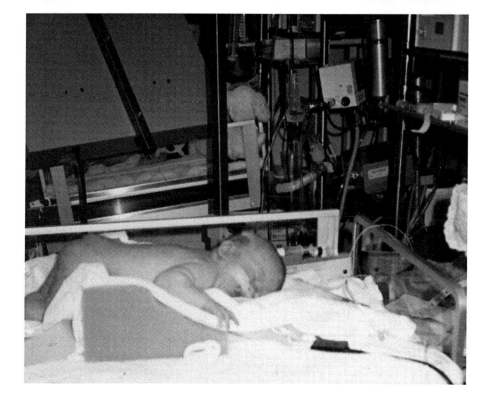

above: NICU *below left:* First Steps *below right:* Preschool Charm

above: Cutting down the Championship net
below left: Motorcycle Man *below right:* Big dreams

above:
Teaching Abby
to "give it all
she's got"

center:
Ice cream time

below:
Three deep

top:
Power Sports

center:
The long, hard road to success is paved with determination.

bottom:
Head of the Family

CHAPTER 6

A Cute Little Kid On Crutches

Song, Song of the South
Sweet 'Tater Pie and Shut (Your) Mouth,
It's Gone and Gone With the Wind
Ain't Nobody Lookin' Back Again.

variation on recording by Alabama[12]

Cody loved and sang that song all of the time in the preschool years. He knew it was supposed to be "shut my mouth" but that was something he rarely did, so I suppose he had trouble singing it too. The last line was true. As hard as things had been to endure to that point, we vowed we would not whine or wallow. We would not look back, but rather we would lunge forward. In fact, this chapter is dedicated almost entirely to fun and progress.

Making the decision to take Cody to PEP was a marvelous change for all of us. The first morning, however, was challenging, as most milestone days are.

I had been taking Cody to the building that housed PEP for a short while already because he had developmental therapy sessions there. That was one of the ways his team learned how curious and compassionate he was. The first therapy session schedule set for Cody was at the same time as an autistic child. The therapy cubicles were divided by wooden screens only. The sessions were thirty minutes. While Cody's therapist was supposed to be teaching him to make decisions that worked toward a goal of self-care (which I thought was a little much for a two-year-old), the autistic child would sit under the table in his cubicle and bang his head on the underside of the table calling continuously for his mom. Of course, they kept him from harming himself, and unlike all other therapy sessions we attended, the parent was asked to remain with the child. A sort of family therapy, I suppose.

It was not long after we started that Cody's sessions had to be changed to a new schedule because he would spend the whole thirty minutes (no matter how hard we tried to divert his attention) telling us, "Y'all better get that boy his mom. That ain't right. What's wrong with y'all? Can't you hear the boy asking for his momma? Y'all should be ashamed. He's going to hurt his head. He needs his momma." On and on and on. No matter how many times we tried to convince him the child was safe and his mom was actually in the room with him, he continued to plead for help for the child. So we moved Cody to a different time.

The advantage to PEP was that his therapist would be there every day while Cody was on the day care side. Not only could she go get him and do his sessions while he was already there (since she had discovered she did not need me), but also she could keep an eye on him for me, especially the first few weeks. Plus, that was one less appointment per week we would have to take him to. We were always grateful for that type of relief.

I was shaky the first morning because we had never left him with anyone outside of family and very close friends—friends like Dot, whom we would trust with our lives and our children. When we drove into the parking lot, I forgot about a big dip in the concrete and hit it hard. Cody wheeled around and looked at me over the edge of his big car seat, big enough to hold him and the braces, and shouted, "You cazy, Momma. You boke my hip."

I assured him, "No, I didn't, Son, but I'm sorry we hit so hard."

He replied, "That's okay, but you a cazy momma." At that moment I thought he was the cutest, most charming little boy in the world. Leaving him with people I barely knew was going to be heart-breaking. I knew that, but I was still not prepared for what happened.

As we were getting out of the car, I was talking to him about all the neat kids I met when I came to tour the day care and the sweet teachers with fun ideas and planned activities. Since the neurosurgeon's instructions of caution, my work schedule, and all the surgeries and recoveries had greatly limited his exposure to other children, I wanted to make sure that he knew if other children bothered him, he could not just punch them. He loved to watch wrestling, and I was afraid he would

above left: Little Fiddler *above right:* Challenger Baseball *below:* The Champ

above: Wheelchair Basketball
below left: Singin' "Song of the South" *below right:* Mr. Charm and Personality

try to put some of those moves into action. He assured me he understood and truly seemed excited about being with other children. What he must not have understood was that I was actually going to leave him there and go to work.

He went right in and started to play with the other children his age. They stared a little at the braces and crutches, something I had dreaded, but it only lasted for a moment. I was so relieved. The whole philosophy of PEP was to facilitate the acceptance of children with disabilities by normal kids, and you could tell it. I was relieved, thinking the separation was going to go smoothly. Boy, was I wrong. Even though I worked at a day care center for the first three years of college and I was fully aware that you could never assume that a toddler understands completely what you have told him, after everything Cody had dealt with, I believed he could. False. I knelt beside him and kissed him on the cheek and told him, "Bye, Baby. Mom is going to work now. I love you. They will take very good care of you. Have fun and I will pick you up as soon as I get off work." He came unglued. He started crying and begging me not to leave him. Immediately the teachers started telling me to go quickly, and he would be fine. *How did they know? They didn't know him.* I was a wreck. I had lost a full night's sleep the night before, worrying and praying, hoping this would not happen.

They were pushing me out the door and Cody was lying on the floor, holding to the hem of my scrub pants, screaming, "Don't leave me. I'll die up here. Kids die here every day. Tell Daddy to come up here. They won't take care of me. They will let me fall and get hurt. Please don't go." I forced myself to the car. His assigned teacher, a very sweet lady we still keep in touch with, was trying to hold him in her lap. I was horrified as I started the car and drove off. I cried so hard all the way to work I had to stop twice and regain my composure just to be able to see. At every traffic light, I wanted to go back, get him, and go home. I just kept thinking of all the wonderful references and recommendations I had gotten on PEP. Also, at the hospital they had changed my schedule because the forty-hour work weekends had become unbearable, and they really wanted me to go back into the supervisory position that I had given up when Cody was born. Great ideas for both of us. He needed social skills, and I needed weekends off so our family could go to ball games, movies, etc.—something besides work and medical care.

My heart was torn. I was frightened and confused, feelings I was familiar with, but did not want to have.

When I arrived at the hospital, it was all I could do to go inside. My closest colleagues were waiting. They knew I was going to be upset about leaving him, but I am not sure they were prepared for that degree of upset. In the setting where I worked, most of my co-workers were also very dear friends. Most of them had small children and had already lived through the "first day" separation horror. They were a great comfort to be around. As soon as I recovered enough, I called PEP. I was so happy when I heard his therapist's voice on the other end of the line. My first and only question was, "Is Cody okay?"

Her response astounded me because she knew both of us so well. She said, "What do you mean?"

"Well, when I left him he was screaming and begging me not to go."

Her surprised response was, "What time was that?"

"Six forty-five," I answered through more tears.

She laughed and announced, "Baby, that was all an act for you. I got here at 8 A.M., and he was running the place."

I stopped crying, thanked her after she reassured me she would watch out for him, and hung up. That little monkey. That morning's show emphasized something that still holds true today. Along with being charming, he is the master of manipulation. God help us!

Cody tried a few more maneuvers to alter the day care scene but soon began to adjust beautifully. As would become a lifelong habit of his, he developed a crush on his teacher and some close friendships with the kids. For two years, he became King of PEP. He was so funny. He sang and told jokes all of the time. There were a few more surgeries, but we dealt with them and our five doctors well. My whole family had become pros at dealing with spica casts, braces, walkers, and crutches—all of it.

On one occasion, Cody was scheduled to do his annual tests to make sure his kidneys were functioning properly. He and I took two days off because three tests were required, an IVP which required an IV and dye, an ultrasound which was simple, and a triple renal function test that requires nuclear medicine and lying flat on a table perfectly still for one hour, not something most three year olds can or will do. I thought, *If spina bifida is not a trip around the world, I don't know what is.*

By this time, I had learned very well how to manipulate by bribery, and Cody had learned how to take full advantage of every medical ordeal to retrieve his latest desires. Mr. Charm and Personality kept in his room at all times a copy of, not coloring books or books to read and look at pictures like other kids his age, but the latest Toys R Us sale paper. He even called it Toys *For* Us. We never corrected him because it seemed so appropriate. He always reminded me, upon my complaining that his toy expenditures were draining us, that he only picked from what was on sale. Like I said earlier, he is the master of manipulation.

On that particular occasion, his heart's desire was a BatMobile. Of course, he explained to me in no uncertain preschooler terms that it would be no fun without the figures of Batman, Robin, Joker, and whomever else he could remember to name. Still, we made the deal going in. One of the most helpful aspects of our mother/son relationship was that I had agreed to never tell him a lie about what was going on, and he agreed, in turn, to always express his true feelings and be as brave as he could possibly be. I kept my promise about 99 percent of the time. Only on a couple of occasions did we keep the truth from him and then only because we believed the details would terrify him and create a less than optimal outcome.

Thank God, part of being a Christian is being honest and creating a relationship with your children based on love and respect. Cody and I have such a healthy relationship to this day because of love and honesty. At times, now, he will come to me and say, "Mom, I need to talk to you about something I don't want to share with anyone else." When he does that, I am always so thankful for the early days when I was honest with him and encouraged him to trust me, because those are always things he really needs to say or get advice on. Living with a disability like spina bifida, CP, etc., is so difficult, but I can only imagine how much more challenging it is if the child does not have someone who loves him to confide in. Cody tells me often how glad he is to have that. He kept his part of the bargain 100 percent of the time, always brave, so brave, and on top of that, kind. We often recited the Golden Rule reduced to this, "Treat other people the way you want to be treated." That worked for us.

Thank goodness, the people doing the various tests those two days were pleasant people because Cody was a little comedian, and there were times when health care workers were not amused. However, before those two days were done, he had managed to entertain the staff of several departments of the hospital.

We began with the easy one, the ultrasound. The test only took a few minutes, was non-invasive, and the lady conducting the scan was very kind. The only problem was that Cody was nervous, so he chattered and sang, etc., more than usual, and the lady was immediately charmed by him. Thus I had to drag him away when she was done so we could move on to our next test and so could she.

The second stage was the 'nuclear medicine' one, lying perfectly flat and still for a one-hour test. I was really in a state of dread as we approached that department. When we entered, we discovered that Cody was the only patient there. I'm not sure if they had cleared their calendar for the incoming big, bad preschooler or what, but I was thankful by the end of that ordeal that we were alone. After giving the nuclear med, they instructed me to get a chair from fifteen feet away so I could sit by him at the right level and try to keep him still for an hour. They laid him on the table and began to talk to him about the importance of not moving at all during that test, as I was dragging this heavy wooden chair over to the table. Well, unfortunately, the legs made a grating sound as they drug and Mr. Cute sat up abruptly and yelled out, "Mom, did you poot?" That broke the place up. I was so embarrassed and the staff could not quit laughing.

All I said was, "It's going to be a long hour, huh?" We got through it and for years when we would return to that facility for medical care, I would see one of them in the hall and they would snicker. It was one of those "out of the mouths of babes" episodes. At the end, they gave me instructions on careful disposal of his diapers because they were radioactive. Some events wind up giving you more information than you care to think about. It almost sounded like 'sci-fi' to me.

On the second morning, we went early to face the dreaded IVP. On the way that morning, in the car, we renewed the terms of our bargain. He would be brave during the stick and the dye, and I would head straight for the BatMobile store as soon as the test was completed.

We arrived to find two people assigned to assist him with the trial. They used the tiniest needle possible, found a vein without difficulty, and made it past the stick with only a big grimace. The procedure requires the injection of the dye, a thirty-minute wait for it to circulate through the kidneys, and then the films can be made. There had been a big goof on my part. I had forgotten, in my effort to ease us past the stick, to tell Cody about the thirty-minute wait. As soon as the dye was injected and needle removed, he jumped down off the table to everyone's amazement and exclaimed to them while jerking my hand, "That's it! I'm history; I'm out of here! See ya. I'm gone to the Batmobile store."

I snapped back, "Whoa, Pal. Baby, you have to give the dye thirty minutes to work and then take the x-rays."

He countered with, "Oh, no ma'am. You said if I would be brave for the dye, then that was it. I'm history; I'm out of here. That Batmobile is jumping off the shelf wanting me to buy it. Let's get it in gear."

Back and forth we argued the entire thirty minutes while those ladies literally bent double with laughter. By the time they actually did the films, I felt like I had boxed a ten-round boxing match and lost. I learned a valuable lesson that day about bargaining with a child like him; don't leave out important details. Cody cuts you no slack!

During that time, Paul completed a degree in business at the local university. We were excited about the graduation, and I made the thirty-mile trip to retrieve Mamaw and return her so she could watch her grandson receive his diploma. Somehow, Mamaw, Cody, and I were separated from the rest of the family. Since Paul had to be with the graduates the entire time, I was left with the task of getting Cody, in braces and arm crutches, and Paul's 80-year-old grandmother across the street from the parking lot to the place for the ceremony in heavy traffic. We met the challenge well, even though I was sweating profusely, and both of them were complaining. However, when they suddenly found themselves at the bottom of the coliseum steps, about twenty-five of them, they both balked. So as I have had to do so often throughout his life, I took a deep breath, told Cody to hold tight to his crutches and Mamaw to her purse, picked my braced-up son and his crutches up in my left arm, took Mamaw's left hand in my right hand, and with great difficulty, climbed that steep staircase. When we reached the top, I felt like I had been in training for mountain climbing. They both appeared to be exhausted; I am not sure from what.

Performing a feat like that is often possible only once in a lifetime. I felt as if that had been it. The trouble was that we would somehow need to get back to the car. I determined to, and did, pray for the answer while inside.

When we got inside, a sweet lady, a total stranger to us but obviously one of God's angels, asked some people to move up one row so we could sit on a level row and not do any more climbing. I am not sure if they knew her or if our appearance scared them, but they gladly obliged. Our helper sat by us and told me all about her son who was graduating and going on to law school. The intermittent conversation helped to break up the boring task of watching 500 people, graduate and undergraduate school students, receive their degrees. Cody and Mamaw actually seized that opportunity to take a nap, and I was glad. I woke them just before Paul walked across the stage.

When the ceremony was over, I did not even attempt to find Paul in that huge crowd with those two in tow. He had his own car and knew where to meet us for the celebration meal. Besides, God had sent this new friend to help us, and without a request to do so, she volunteered to stay with Cody on the outside platform of the coliseum while I assisted Mamaw back down that steep staircase. After the climb up and his nap, Cody acted as though he was perfectly content to remain with that charming lady until we could return to help him to the car. As it turned out, the key word was acted. Actually, she and I were both scared to leave him, not really knowing that lady well, so we tried to rush. Rushing through that maze of people with an elderly lady, driving out of a packed parking lot into bumper-to-bumper traffic and back around to where they were, was quite a chore. Still, out of fear, we did it in record time.

I am here to tell you, Mr. Charm and Personality had a surprise waiting for me upon my return. No, he had not been kidnapped or harmed. Instead, he was sitting on the bottom step with a police officer on each side of him, and the moment I saw them, I knew I was in for a treat. True to my expectations, as soon as I stepped out of the car Cody began the dog and pony show. "What is wrong with you? Don't you know you are not supposed to leave little children by themselves? You didn't really know that lady, and I am handicapped anyway. Anything could have happened. Thank the Lord, these nice policemen came along and rescued me." The police officers just sat and stared at me without expression.

My only comment to him was, "Let's go." I was not going to feed into that little performance. My words to the police officers were, "No child on earth is more loved or cared for. I was just in a predicament and a nice lady offered to help me. I would never knowingly put him in danger." They both kept that solemn expression but after spending ten minutes with him, I am sure they were hopeful of my return. He probably reminded them of *The Ransom of Red Chief,* a movie where kidnappers after ransom money actually paid a child's family to take him back. I am sure we provided their entertainment at dinner that night. It was most definitely the hit story of Paul's graduation party.

That same night, because we had some overnight guests here for the graduation, it was determined that Cody would stay next door at my mother's house. Cody packed a little suitcase he had begged for that read *Going to Grandma's.* His baggage consisted of pajamas, chocolate chip cookies, his toothbrush, and a copy of *Little Red Riding Hood,* which was his favorite story at that time.

My mom is a very early riser and an "early to bed" person. She also is the queen of snoring. Cody, on the other hand, likes to stay up late. However, due to the strong, loving bond between them, they often adjusted to each other's schedules. Late that night I went to check on Cody after our guests had gone to bed. As I approached Mom's bedroom, I heard snoring and sobbing in a sort of rhythm. I was alarmed, especially when I got close enough to see Cody sitting up in the bed crying, looking very frightened. I rushed in and picked him up. He immediately wrapped his arms around my neck and I pleaded with him, "Tell Momma what's wrong, Son. Did something scare you? Did you have a bad dream?" After what seemed like a long time had passed and I had reassured him several times that his mom was there and nothing was going to harm him, I asked again, "Please tell me what scared you so much?"

Finally, he raised his head, pointed to my mother, and replied with sincerity, "Ma's the wolf." I held him close, trying not to chuckle and take a chance on his thinking I did not take his fear seriously, but it was hard not to laugh thinking that he had awakened after dreaming about the *Little Red Riding Hood* story, heard Ma's snoring, and surmised that his grandmother had also been eaten by the wolf. Believing he was alone with a grandmother-eating wolf must have been terrifying. I woke Ma up and together we finally convinced him his fear was unfounded. After about an hour, he fell asleep again. That late night adventure has provided fun for many people over the years, including him and Ma.

We took some wonderful family trips during those preschool years. That was the only time in our lives we were able to travel in the off-season. That worked well for us. We took a trip to Arizona and New Mexico, the Grand Canyon, and Sedona. We took pictures of Cody there, and when our family members and friends saw him sitting on the edge of the canyon and splashing in the middle of Red Rock Crossing, they had a fit. We weren't afraid. Our only fear was the same then as it is now—that his life would be totally consumed with medical care and that he would not have a full life. I wanted to show him the world, and I wanted to prove to all the negative people that the "poor little crippled child" attitude was a roadblock to so many kids and to their potential to accomplish great things. With God's help, we did just that.

Between the age of 2 and 4, Cody grew in size and stature. He talked extremely well and began to develop many interests. He entertained everyone around him, and we received an array of suggestions for his future, which ranged from on stage comedian to gubernatorial candidacy. He told jokes, too, and he shook the hands of everyone he met. Dr. J. was even scratching his head in amazement. Even though Cody's head measurement stayed above the normal curve and his CT scans were all abnormal, he was thriving.

One of Cody's interests was swimming. That pleased the whole family, especially since Ma and Cheryl had a pool in their back yard right next door. He loved both of them dearly and spent a great deal of time there. He spent a lot of time in the pool with arm floaties on and all of us soon realized that, as usual, spina bifida kids are in an extra degree of danger. We learned quickly that Dr. J.'s warnings of skin and wound troubles were real. When Cody got even a small scrape on his foot from concrete, it would take from six months to a year to heal. Paralysis is a monster. We avoided many crises by putting indoor/outdoor carpet around the shallow end of the pool. Since he was forced to crawl when out of his braces that was a lifesaver.

During the summer of his third year, we decided to give him swimming lessons. Dr. D. had told me that swimming was the number one recommended exercise for spina bifida kids, so I wanted him to learn the proper way to swim. It just so happened that a friend's parents lived two streets over, had a pool, and she taught lessons there. As always, we were concerned about kids staring and laughing at him. She called one day and said she was going to have a class for him and two other children. The other two kids were very frightened of water, and she felt they would make a trio that would help each other. I love it when people are sensitive like that. When I revealed the plan, everyone was excited except Cody. He knew the teacher and liked her a lot, but when he was told we could not stay during the lessons, he was terrified. Bribe time again.

So after the promise of his latest wish being fulfilled upon completion of the class, we drove there on Monday for the first of nine lessons. It was always impossible to predict or prepare for Cody's reactions to new activities. We arrived and I rolled him, armed with goggles and a towel, into the back yard where the pool was. The teacher was so glad to see him, but the other children were shy and frightened. I thought Cody would assume his normal leadership role. That didn't happen. Instead, as I turned to leave, he created the same scenario we had gone through on the first day of PEP. He threw himself on the ground, clung to my leg, and begged me not to leave him. Ms. Jen picked him up and forced me to go. I peeped through the bushes at the other end of the house until I could see he was warming up to the whole idea. When I went back to get him an hour later, he was happy and jabbered all the way home about being the class leader.

The second afternoon I expected a smooth transition. Wrong. When the time came for me to depart, he fell to the ground, clinging to my leg exclaiming, "Please don't leave me. It's so dangerous. Kids drown up here every day."

I tried to calm him down, but it wasn't happening. I tried to reason with him by saying, "Son, you are safe. Ms. Jen will watch you closely. There are only three of you; if anyone drowned, I would notice." He wasn't listening.

Ms. Jen instructed, "Good-bye, Mom, and don't sneak around the house to peek." So I left. Kids always work better when parents aren't around. That knowledge was all that made it bearable.

Toward the end of the first week, he was separating with less drama and we were so glad. However, after the weekend off, Monday brought the same scene as day one. On Friday of the second week, a "swim off" was slated. As Paul and I started over there with Cody acting pouty, I told Paul, "Don't expect too much at the swim off because most of what he has done is lie on the ground, crying, and begging me not to leave him." Cody grinned but said nothing. We soon found out why.

We went in and met the other two sets of parents then took seats at the shallow end of the pool. After Ms. Jen helped the other two kids to show what they had learned; it was Cody's turn to solo. He dove off the side of the pool, went to the bottom, and swam all the way to the deep end wall before surfacing. Paul and I were so frantic that our rumps both came up out of our chairs in the fear that he needed rescuing. We were the only people who needed rescuing, from our dramatic child. Swimming came easily after that.

During that same period, music gained a permanent spot in Cody's heart and life. He had been singing and bringing joy to himself and others since he was a few months old. He strummed a mean guitar and played a dynamic drum solo. He loved country and western music and longed to perform publicly.

Once Ma, Cheryl, and I decided to have a rummage sale. From the time we announced our plans for the sale until the day it took place (probably six weeks time), Cody begged his dad and us every day to build him a platform and set up a microphone on a stand so he could perform for the yard sale shoppers. He wore us out. I kept telling him, "Baby, I just don't know any country and western singers that had their debut at a rummage sale." He was appalled. I held my ground because we needed all the room we had on the concrete area to display the items for sale. That day he tried sitting in a chair between two racks of clothes strumming his guitar and singing, but no one seemed to be paying attention to him, much less offering him money or recording contracts. I don't think Cody realized the true goals of rummage sale shoppers. They do help you to void your home of unwanted and dust-catching items, but I don't do very well with people who are being allowed to buy a $350 coat for 50 cents and then they want to know if you will take 25 cents. The other thing, you work your rump off selling and marking and at the end of the day, you look around and wonder what is missing. Of course, there are always the "entire stock" buyers who offer to buy the entire sale's items, valued at $3000 for $40. I was more apt to bag it all up and give it to Goodwill.

Now Paul had worked hard helping us to set up tables, moving heavy objects, running electricity to the table that displayed lamps, coffee pots, etc., and setting up the cash box to enable us to make change. However, we lost him when he and Cody went to the end of our long driveway to hammer the sign into the ground announcing, 'Yard Sale Here' and a group of six people drove by in a ragged truck and all screamed at them in unison, "Ya gonna let us rummage tonight?"

He came rushing back to our house pulling Cody in his red wagon and exclaimed after relating what had happened, "This is not a flea market. This is our home."

So during the sale, when his singing was not the big hit he had hoped, Cody talked Paul into helping him and his friend Bart make a Kool-Aid stand out of cardboard. They also made a gallon of blue Kool-Aid. The sign on the stand read, "Kool-Aid 25 cents." The account I heard from friends who came to the sale was that Bart would hail them down in the drive and send them to Cody at the stand. There he would take their quarter, and in turn, they would receive one half cup of Kool-Aid. He then informed them they could get the cup filled for 25 cents more and sugar added for an additional 10 cents. Later I learned when the Kool-Aid crowd dwindled; they managed to sell rocks from the driveway to some of our closest friends. Needless to say, that was our one and only yard sale.

Since he had no music breakthrough at the yard sale, at around 4 years old, Cody began to take violin lessons. During the first year of violin, the progress was very slow. People who play that instrument will tell you, as the instructor told us—over two hundred different details have to be achieved before a song can be played. Actually, the very first instrument consisted of cardboard and rubber bands. Rhythm exercises, like Mississippi stop-stop, were the first order of learning the art of playing the violin. Well, Cody was Mr. Charm and Personality, but he was a little lacking in the patience department.

When we bought his first real violin, he was so excited and just wanted to rip out a song. When we carefully went over the proper method of removing it from the case, tuning it, setting the bow, etc., he was a little less than amused. At his first recital when he named the parts and squeaked out Mississippi stop-stop, all of us were a little stressed. If Cody had not developed the measure of patience and persistence he needed for his medical care, violin lessons would have been insufferable.

Cody maintained his love for country music, but there are some things you catch onto quickly. Where violin is concerned, the first things you learn are how complicated it is to play and the amount of discipline that is involved, and if you have a true love for the world of violins, you have no tolerance for "fiddlin." At least that was true of the players and teachers we met.

Cody loved to watch and listen to fiddlers. He just learned not to share that with the violinists. One day my mother was watching him after PEP until I could get home from work. As soon as I arrived home that afternoon, I went next door to check on Cody. We had our usual glad reunion, and then Mom wanted to show me something in her bedroom. We talked there for a few minutes and then returned to the family room to discover Cody was not there. Since she and I had left him there watching cartoons and we were the only ones at home, I went into a state of panic. We called his name, no answer. We checked all the rooms in the house, nothing. I ran out the back door to the swimming pool, no Cody (thank God), but I heard a strange sound coming from the side of the house. I walked around there to find an open but empty violin case right outside the door. Across the carport from the side door was a huge pine tree surrounded by flowerbeds and encased with landscape timbers. I peeped around the tree and an amazing sight met my eyes. There was Cody, sitting on the landscape timber, bearing down on that violin, sawing out a close resemblance to a fiddlin' tune and laughing, while horsehair from the bow was flying everywhere.

It was one of those moments when you would give anything to have your movie camera with you. Of course, he fell into fear and trembling when he noticed me and halted, looking shocked. Holding back the laughter, I asked, "What's up, Pal?"

He replied nervously, "Mom, I know what y'all said about being careful with this violin, but I just couldn't take it anymore. Mississippi stop-stop is a dud, even for a four year old. I just had to take things in my own hands and have me a Charlie Daniel's concert. Boy, was it fun!" I had to hug him. Of course, I was upset when I saw the scrapes on the bottom of the violin, where, not having time to coordinate carrying the case with his arm crutches, he had taken it out and crawled from the door to the tree, scraping the instrument across the concrete as he went. So what? Not taking a chance on snuffing out that wonderful personality and creativity was so much more important than the violin and bow repair costs. I am so thankful I did not upset him on that occasion because when things are not going well with his health now, I look back to that day and have a fond memory to make me smile. God bless his little soul. The violin and bow were repaired, and we progressed through several more instruments and teachers. At age 10, he would go on to win the State Fiddlin' Contest in the junior division, and at age 15, he proceeded to be a member of the local youth symphony. He never had to choose; he played both the fiddle and the violin.

Another special event when Cody was four took us a little by surprise. My cousin and his fiancée called and asked if we would consider letting Cody be the ring bearer in their wedding. They told me he was the cutest little boy they had ever seen, and it would be such an honor for him to be part of their wedding. It was a big, fancy wedding in a huge church with lots of attendants. There you go, family not ashamed or inhibited by the disability. What a blessing! The rest of our family was concerned about how to get him down the aisle, while I was concerned about keeping that little motor mouth quiet during the vows. Both were accomplished under the plan we made.

We were all excited as we made the journey to Jackson, Mississippi, where the wedding was to take place. We arrived just in time to make it to the church for the rehearsal. The wedding party was so taken with Cody. It's a shame more handicapped kids do not get a chance to have those experiences.

We left the hotel early the morning of the wedding and went to the tuxedo shop in the mall. When Cody tried on that size 4 tuxedo, it fit perfectly and he looked adorable. The cutest part was his expression. You could tell he thought he was a king. He said, "I am so in love with one of those girls in the wedding, and she is bound to fall for me in these threads." My big, bad preschooler.

The shoes were more complicated. We had tried on every child-sized black patent leather shoe in that place before we found a pair that would go over the braces. Those things are so wide and made of Teflon. Shoes have proven to be a challenge in every stage of his life. There were times when I would buy cute little canvas sneakers and the braces would eat through the sides of them in one day. Couldn't wear them, couldn't return them. It was the same way with crutch tips. There were weeks when the crutches would eat through a set of $6 crutch tips every day, especially when the concrete would "sweat" and Cody and I would slip and slide all the way to the car. Even though it was depressing, those were times we learned not to fall apart over the minor stuff. We learned to put a dime on the end of the crutch to keep the metal end from eating through the tip. Finally, the companies that make crutch tips started putting a metal washer in the same place we had put the dimes. So we left that store armed with black tux, white shirt, black shoes, blue bow tie, and a cumberbund to match the wedding party—and a very happy child.

The wedding was beautiful. Many people cried when the bride walked down the aisle, but they were just as touched when the 6'4" handsome groomsman carried Cody and the ring pillow to the altar. They were both glowing, and Cody's expression when he saw the bride in all her splendor was priceless. After the wedding he told me, "I am in love with Sara; she looked so pretty today."

"She is a pretty little girl."

I was speaking of the flower girl, but he looked stunned, pointed to one of the bridesmaids, and said, "I am talking about that girl."

The young lady he was pointing to was at least twenty years old. My comment was, "Excuse me; I should have known you would not be interested in a girl your age." For years he would constantly develop crushes on older women.

During those preschool years, Cody and Mamaw would create some very comical situations. One of those happened when Cody was

3, at the state fair. Now having a good time at the fair, while pushing a child in a jogging stroller over all of those cords, was a challenge. The blessing for us was that Cody could make anything fun. To our surprise, the big laughs would come in the exhibit building and in the petting zoo. We were making our way around the fair, fighting the stroller/cord issue, and we overheard some people talking about the petting zoo. I told Paul, "Let's go there. The cords are wearing us out, he is too little to ride the rides he likes or play the games, and there won't be any cords in there." Every one jumped at that idea, but none of us was prepared for the adventure awaiting.

When we reached the petting zoo, we were astonished to find the animals were not in stalls or cages. The fair workers would allow a few people at one time into a gate, after selling you cups of animal food, and there you were greeted by an array of animals, very hungry animals. The group consisted of lambs, sheep, goats of all sizes, lamas, donkeys, geese, etc. It was a unique but hilarious arrangement, and zoo was a perfect name for it. We provided extra entertainment for everyone around us, compliments of Cody and Mamaw. Although they asked people to leave the strollers outside the gate, due to his inability to walk, they allowed Cody to stay in his. Mamaw had worn a trench coat with the belt hanging down on both ends. As soon as we entered that gate, it became obvious those baby goats thought the seat cover on the stroller and Mamaw's belt would make a gourmet meal. It was ridiculous; the goats were charging us, and we were practically throwing the cups of food at them, which made the larger animals charge us to get the food and eat cups and all. Cody was laughing but begging us to get them off of him, and Mamaw was slapping at them and screaming, "Get away, get away you scoundrels," followed by, "Let's get the heck out of here; those devils are going to eat the baby!" We escaped there with child, stroller, and belt still intact somehow.

Next we went into the building where the displays were. The hall went in a circle. No sooner had we escaped the man-eating goats, laughed it off, and entered to view the first exhibit, than two loose adult goats went flying by, circling the hall, while bleating loudly. Mamaw fell apart and exclaimed, "My God, those devils are everywhere! I bet you when I catch them they will think bleat!"

I took charge and commanded, "You are not chasing any goats.

They have employees here to do that. Let's go, I've seen enough. I didn't know how easy fighting cords was." Needless to say, I was glad to escape with our health, but they had created a "remember forever" night at the State Fair.

Cody and Mamaw made a comical pair as long as she lived, and they loved each other dearly. On one occasion, Paul had gone and picked her up to visit with us for the weekend, and as they pulled into the driveway, they noticed Cody making his way across the yard with his little walker. When they reached our house, Cody had not even looked at them, and she immediately inquired, "Where is he going and why is that white bag hanging on his walker?"

I explained, "He got angry with me and told me he was leaving home. In the bag, he has a toy gun for protection and chocolate chip cookies for nourishment. I told him to go ahead. Don't worry; he will be back for supper." She was irate and had Paul go bring him back right then. Not many people, including Mamaw, can comprehend being thankful for normal experiences like a kid "running away from home" episode.

As Mamaw grew less able to care for herself, my sister-in-law and I began to take turns going to her house and helping her clean, buy groceries, and go to the doctor. One Saturday Christie and I went together to do a major house cleaning, and we took Paul and Sonny along to help with heavy jobs. Cody and Jamie, our niece, were also with us. Mamaw's house was surrounded by pastureland, so we told the kids they could play outside and made them promise not to go near the road. Sonny and Paul were supposed to be policing them, which apparently did not happen. Paul came to the door in the middle of our major cleaning and said, "Y'all come look at the children." None of the three of us were expecting what we saw. There was an old donkey loping across the pasture with Jamie and Cody riding him, while laughing all the way. Cody, in a full set of braces, was behind Jamie, riding that old donkey without a saddle. Apparently, they crawled under a barbed-wire fence, picked apples from another elderly couple's apple tree to entice the donkey, helped each other up on his back, shed Cody's crutches, and spurred that donkey on as if they were in the Wild West. Mamaw had a fit, proclaiming her neighbors would shoot them, while the rest of us had a belly laugh. We did make them come in after a few minutes, and we explained trespassing to them. They were scared, but they had truly enjoyed that ride.

About two months later, I picked up the phone and overheard Jamie telling Cody, "The last two times I went to Mamaw's I didn't see that donkey. I think we killed him." Later I assured them that although Mamaw had made a big dramatic scene about the donkey being too old to ride, I had seen him since, and he was fine.

The two years Cody went to PEP helped him to develop in many ways. He learned much about interacting with other children and about teacher/student relationships. He had been well accepted there, but one day, right after his fourth birthday, Cody arrived home exclaiming, "I don't like day care anymore. I want to go to school."

I asked, "Why don't you like day care anymore?" I was afraid he had experienced something there that made him unhappy.

He replied, " 'Cause, all that goes there is a bunch of babies."

I declared, "Yes, Son, that is the purpose of day care. I am not sure you can go to school at four."

His comeback was, "Y'all will be sorry. It's a dangerous place. For instance, that bin of beans and rice they have, those suckers eat a big mouth full of that every few minutes. One of them is always choking. Plus, they pull drowned kids from their pool all the time." Well, I know when I am in a battle I cannot win. I knew of no choking episodes, and the pool was a small plastic wading pool guarded by three workers anytime children were in it.

Still, his message was clear. I would now have a new mission—finding a preschool that would accept him. I was stupefied by the challenge that turned out to be.

CHAPTER 7

Mainstreaming a Physically-Challenged Child— In School and In Life

So many times I've questioned
Certain circumstances of things I could not understand,
And many times in trials a weakness blurs my vision,
Then my frustration gets so out of hand.
It is then I am reminded I've never been forsaken,
I've never had to stand one test alone;
As I look at all my victories, the spirit rises up in me
And it's through the fire my weakness is made strong.

Chorus:
He never promised that the cross would not get heavy
And the hill would not be hard to climb.
He never offered our victories without fighting,
but He said help would always come in time.
So just remember when you're standing in the valley of decision
And the adversary says, "Give in."
Just hold on; Our Lord will show up
And He will take you through the fire again.

Words to "Through the Fire"
sung by the Crabb family[13]

The search for a preschool turned out to be more challenging than the day care search, but for an entirely different reason. Believe it or not, he could not qualify because he did not have *enough* problems. More like, his problems were not in the right category. He was too smart! Praise the Lord! That was our first experience at being over-qualified for anything. Amazingly, the law requires every child to go to kindergarten but the preschoolers, at least in our area at that time, were limited to those who scored poorly enough on an evaluation test to need a head start. They even called the preschool program Head Start. One thing became increasingly clear about our son, when he made up his mind about something within reason, within reach, we could either find a path to it or go on to get psychiatric therapy. So after much prayer, reluctantly, we went to talk to the teacher of what was then called "special ed" in the school he was zoned for.

It's amazing how terms change and so many people feel that lightens the load. True enough, some terms do not have the harshness or darkness that others do. For instance, "physically challenged" beats the heck out of the word "crippled." In the end, though, we found that one of the very best things you can do for children is to teach them to accept their limitations and be proud of their abilities. Teach them not to be ashamed but view it as a little inconvenience. That attitude always inspires others. Overprotection and love are not synonymous. What actually happens is that their abilities and gifts are stifled. They usually get the idea that the reason you keep them in and won't let them do any outside activities is that you are ashamed of their disability. Then they become ashamed as if they have done something wrong. Communication is the key to raising kids successfully in all cases. You just cannot know what young people are thinking about adversity if you don't ask. If you go through a divorce and never discuss it with the children, they think it is their fault. If one parent dies and the kids don't get to air their feelings, they believe some horrible wish made during an argument or a bad act of theirs caused the death of the beloved parent. It is the same with disabilities.

Spina bifida is not something we would have chosen, but we sure don't shy away from talking about it. Because of that, Cody has a clear understanding of it and talks openly without burdens of shame or guilt. That is such a blessing, and it helps everyone around him to be comfortable with him. There are times when you must fight fire with fire. The way we dealt with all the staring was not to run and hide.

Instead, we bought bright orange crutches and toxic green wheelchairs and gave people something to stare at.

I was concerned about how well Cody would do in public school. Still, I believed he would be a strong enough, brave enough boy to conquer whatever obstacles he had to. We landed in the preschool of the school he was zoned for. Due to his not qualifying for the Head Start program, special education preschool was our only option. When I went to the school and met the teacher, she was very impressive. She told me that even though there were some mentally challenged kids there, several had physical impairments only. One of the kids coming had been in the NICU with Cody. However, when Cody was discharged after two weeks there that child was not able to go home for fourteen months. That child had a lot of problems and was very small. The teacher would have ten children in the class and would have three teacher's aids. They had some wonderful books, toys, and educational activity tools. Best of all, they had computers. I expected Cody to take right to that, and he did.

When I left him there on the first day, he was a little anxious, but PEP had conditioned him to the morning separations. In addition, even though his PEP caregivers cried on his last day there, he seemed happy to be moving on. His new teacher was really cute and personable, and he formed an immediate attachment to her. She liked him too, and she still keeps up with him and rejoices and cries over his accomplishments to this day. She was one of the great blessings in our lives.

On our first Monday departure, I pondered some things on my way to work. First, in spite of everything, Cody was going to go to school and grow up. Next, we would not be able to check on him as easily as we did at day care nor protect him from staring, teasing, etc., as well as we had in the past. PEP had been designed to promote acceptance of children with disabilities by the kids who were not physically challenged, but we were about to blaze a long and difficult trail by mainstreaming a physically challenged child into the public school system. Like everything else, we prayed our way through, one problem at a time.

When I arrived to pick him up on that first day, he seemed content. He showed me the computer, his desk, locker, and nap area, his drawings, etc., gave the teacher a big hug, and we left. On the way home I asked, "Was your first day fun? Did Ms. H. spend a lot of time with you?" I had the full expectation of his answering yes to both questions.

Instead, he replied with the tone and sarcasm of a senior citizen, "Naw, she spent all day chasing that baby."

I asked in a puzzled voice, "What baby?" When he gave the description, I realized he was talking about the child who had the four-teen-month NICU stay. I worked hard not to chuckle as I told him, "Honey, he's not a baby. He is your age, but he was a lot sicker than you."

His reply was, "The little devil I am talking about is a toddler with a bib on." I knew then there was no convincing him otherwise, so we moved on to other topics. Overall, his first school day had been a blast.

Cody thrived in preschool. He was walking better and better in braces with arm crutches, and he loved the computer activities. He grew very close to the teachers, the aides, and the other kids. He also learned the pledge to the flag and some other school disciplines that made him seem even more mature than before.

The most outstanding story of that year is about him and a little girl named Jess. She did not move her right side well at all. She had been born in a different state and her mother said the doctors had told them she suffered a stroke at birth. She was very cute, but she was extremely shy. Cody was always trying to talk her out of that shyness. Mr. Motor Mouth always felt it was his mission to help every person he met to be friendly and talkative. Jess wanted no part of that. One afternoon I picked Cody up and his report was, "I don't like Jess." I asked why, thinking that he would blame her shyness. To my surprise, he said, "Because she won't move her right arm."

I was startled and immediately explained to him, "Baby, it isn't that she won't move her arm; it's that she can't move that arm, and that is really not a good reason to not like her." He appeared to be angered by my statement and withdrew into deep thought. We rode in silence for a few minutes, and then he stated very emphatically, "That's a bunch of bull. She could move that arm if she wanted to!" Well, far be it from me to discourage the therapist in him. I did, however, feel sorry for Jess knowing little Mr. Stand-back-from-nothing was on her case.

Now lo and behold if Jess didn't get sick and visit a local doctor, one who was not convinced of her "stroke at birth" diagnosis. He
ordered a CT scan. The scan revealed a benign brain tumor. She was
sent to a big medical center where the tumor was removed and confirmed as benign. After a few months of physical therapy, all of her
physical impairments disappeared. What a miracle! She never returned
to preschool, and when Cody inquired about her, I told him her story.
He got this sort of angry look on his face and exclaimed in a loud tone,
"See, I told you she could move that arm if she wanted to!" To God be
the glory, but just that once I let my little encourager think he played
a big part in her recovery. It served him well because he has inspired
many kids since then to develop to their potential.

Cody was the star of preschool, and during that same period,
some activities developed in the community that helped him to form
connections to people who would love and assist him from that point on.
A very important part of that was being appointed as the local Ambassador for the March of Dimes. Once they latched on to him, he had that
job for the next three years. Entertaining crowds while soliciting help
for researchers hoping to find the answers to preventing birth defects
like spina bifida was a great experience for the entire family. His Aunt
Cheryl has a real talent for organizing telethons, fund-raisers, etc. They
became very close during that time. One of the Ambassador duties
was to attend, as a special guest, the "kick-off" breakfast each year for
the March of Dimes campaign. Since Cheryl was a good friend of the
person in charge of that, she suggested bringing in the head basketball coach from the local university. As far as Cody was concerned, he
was an international star. When we entered the top-floor dining room
of that exclusive country club that morning, the coach was the first person Cody spotted and exclaimed loudly, "There's Coach Mike V." The
coach would tell me several years later that Cody stole his heart in that
moment, and they have been close all these years.

That morning the coach was introduced, and as he rose to go to
the speaking platform, he pulled a basketball signed by all the players
from under the table. He presented that to Cody and announced that
Cody would become "Coach Cody" and would have a spot on the bench
with the players at all the college home basketball games that season.
During those few minutes, Cody had one of those facial expressions you

want to preserve for all time. It was one of the memories that help us to survive the awful times. True to Coach V's word, Cody was allowed to sit on the bench that season, as well as for the next twelve years. Plus, one of the 6'10" players carried him in and out of the locker room. Lord knows what he saw and heard in there, but it was not the type of thing I was allowed to monitor. He was also held up by that same huge player at the end of winning the championship game to cut the net off the goal and get a strand of that net. What a marvel all of that was, and I love to go back and look at those pictures. That huge muscular guy in a basketball uniform holding up this little four-year-old with his haircut tapering off to a duck tail, in long leg braces, cutting that net down. Spina bifida is a very damaging birth defect that brings a lot of anguish into the lives of the family involved, but because of his handicap, Cody was also allowed some experiences that any other kid would perish for.

He had some neighborhood incidents at that age too, episodes that gave him a chance to exhibit the leadership abilities he had acquired in preschool. (Some of those I was not so sure would serve him in a positive manner. . . .)

One day my elderly neighbor called me on the phone and reported, "Honey, I hate to tell on Cody, but he and his little girlfriend from across the street are going around the neighborhood selling a set of books y'all bought him about animals."

"You have got to be kidding. They are supposed to be watching a movie over at Ma's house. How much are they selling them for? I hope you didn't buy one."

"Well, that really might be his calling because before I knew it I had bought two because he said one was $7 but I could get two for $10. The little girl is just carrying them for him and smiling. Don't fuss at them; they are too cute. I was just afraid he would get run over on those crutches, and you would be upset about the books."

My answer was, "That may be Mr. Cute's calling later on, but right now his calling is to get home, and I will have him bring your money back to you and retrieve the books. I am sorry. Ma must have let them sneak away from her. He is good at that."

When we located them, Cody was so disappointed that I was not proud of the money he had generated for the family, and he was devastated when he learned he would have to give it back. The little girl was his age and was in love with him. He could have talked her and her younger sister into just about anything.

They proved that one afternoon when I was watching them ride battery-powered four-wheelers over our five-acre lot, and all three of them disappeared. I panicked and ran into Ma's house to implore the assistance of Paul, Ma, and Cheryl to find them. We all spread out, calling their names loudly. Relief came when we discovered they were not in the swimming pool nor drainage canal that ran down the backside of our property. I remember thinking, *Where in the world are they? Surely, no one would kidnap all three of them and those big, heavy four-wheelers. Lord, please bring them home.* After combing every inch of our property and both houses, there was nothing to do but spread out over the neighborhood. We knew that would alarm the girls' parents and all of our elderly neighbors as well. With no other choice, we made a team plan and spread out. Paul located the four-wheelers in the backyard of the neighbor's house to the right of Ma and all three of the kids inside an old school bus they used for storage. The humming sound of those four-wheelers headed toward our house was the sweetest sound I could ever remember hearing. Paul explained that even after finding the riding toys, he could not get the kids to answer his calls. He was forced to get Ms. P., the little lady that lived there, to go in the bus with him to find them. As they all sat there together on the sofa, looking like three little sad stooges, I inquired in an angry voice, "Cody, why didn't you answer Daddy when he was calling you? Y'all scared us to death!"

He was silent for a moment and then replied, "'Cause I didn't want y'all to know we were in there." Well, okay. He had at least been honest. Paul stormed outside in an effort to calm down. As soon as he shut the door Cody whispered, "It was neat in there, Mom. They had a guitar, mattress, all sorts of neat things." It was really hard to be mad at him. Thank goodness that was one of the few times he was ever lost.

One of the most difficult memories of that period for me is a recurring dream that haunted me for several years. For most people it would have been a wonderful dream. For me it was a nightmare. It consisted of Cody and me in a beautiful, fragrant field of wild flowers. Cody was barefooted, and he would run toward me with both arms spread wide, giggling, until he reached me, and I would grab him in my arms and swing him around. We would laugh aloud as we swung around. The nightmare part was I would wake up and realize it was never going to happen, not in this life, not without a miracle from God. I tried to tell myself it was just a glimpse of Heaven presenting as a dream, but it occurred every week for years.

Sadly, that dream would later lead me to make the worst decision of Cody's life. I learned several things from that. One is dreams are dreams and are brought on by anything from suppressed thoughts to indigestion from eating too much of a "blooming onion." Letting dreams shape your life is usually a big mistake. I also learned what a horrible turn of events could result from pride and from not listening to your health care team. The main lesson I unearthed was that you couldn't change the plan God had for your life. You can't make disabilities disappear. God can, but you can't. If you don't accept your limitations with good grace, your life will just be one big frustration and you will never discover what your real purpose is in this life. Trying to make that dream a reality would create a three-year tragedy, take away Cody's ability to ever walk much again—even on crutches, and almost send me to the funny farm. I learned to leave dreams alone after you wake from them. Working toward goals you set for your life while awake and alert is so much better. I kept praying that dream would go away, and it finally did.

When it came time to sign up for kindergarten, we had some reservations about the school for which Cody was zoned. The zoning process had been altered to meet the demands of certain activist groups. The people surrounding us for two miles were middle-class professional people. We knew most of them, and they had morals and standards similar to ours. Due to the zoning, over 50 percent of the students assigned to that school were of the lowest socioeconomic class in town. Many of the children's families were accustomed to very foul language and low morality. I believe in loving all people, but I was afraid of the influence that environment might have on Cody. We never wanted to overprotect him, but my fear was that by putting him in a place with kids who did not have respect for each other nor for the teachers would make him open game for all type of ludicrous remarks and treatment. I decided to seek help from the staff of a private "Christian" school. Once again, I would learn a valuable lesson to be careful because things are rarely what they appear to be. I had some dear friends whose kids went to that school, and they assured me the staff members there were Christian people who would go all out to help me. I realized later those people had children who were not handicapped, and who were overachievers academically, and that the professions of my friends allowed them to give freely of their money. There was another Christian school to consider too, but it was a long distance from our house, and I did not see a way to get him there every day without great difficulty.

Therefore, I made a morning appointment with the principal at the Christian school nearby. When I arrived a few minutes before my appointment time, I was greeted by an assistant principle. The man used only minimal courtesy and right in the middle of pouring my heart out about Cody he said, "Does he read? All of our kindergarteners are already reading." I assured him Cody could read some and tried to finish my story. When I came to explaining his disability, or rather his inability to climb stairs, he immediately cut into me with the words, "We can't help him. All of our classes are upstairs with no elevator." What a rude, uncaring man he was.

For some stupid reason, I decided to try my plea with the principal. When I asked for her, he directed me to her office to wait for what he said was the completion of a meeting. She arrived a few minutes later. Her hair was in perfect form, her clothes would have stood up by themselves they were so stiff, and she greeted me as warmly as an ice storm. Obviously, her rude assistant had warned her why I was there. She cut to the chase, and let me know in no uncertain words that theirs was not the facility for Cody. Even though it was August, there was a definite chill in the air. Following that conversation, I determined that Cody would be much better off where he was zoned. We would deal with the influences as episodes occurred. I shook that woman's cold hand, thanked her, and told her I wanted to make one small suggestion for their school that had nothing to do with disabilities. It turned out to be the only thing I said the whole time that she was interested in. However, her expression turned really sour when I let her know it was to take the word 'Christian' off the front of the school. I let her know we would find some Christian people to help us, and I left.

Over the next few weeks, she left several messages on my answering machine, asking me to call her. Maybe I should have called, but it was time for school to start and we had to move forward. I suspected that my friends had talked to her about us and her treatment of us. Plus, if she wanted a confrontation, I was not interested. I knew the American's with Disabilities Act was passed that year and what it mandated. We could have made demands, but you have to pick your battles. That was one we chose to leave alone. It might have resulted in Cody's being treated badly, and it was not worth the risk.

We decided to go past the two schools closer to our home and enroll Cody in the school he was zoned for. We would fight whatever challenges we had to when they came along. It turned out that we had some issues to face ahead that would change the attitudes of many people. As usual, most of the time it is hard to know what life has in store until you get there.

The first assignment we had was to meet with a group to create what is called an IEP, which stands for Individual Educational Plan, something we would be doing twice a year for the next thirteen years. It was one of many helpful things we would discover that had been implemented into the public school system. The meeting was with his teacher, his principal, a member of the school board, the therapists who would be working with Cody at school, and me. The purpose was to set a schedule that lost minimal class time and identified goals for the therapists and Cody to strive toward for that half of the year. That was our first knowledge of adaptive physical education teachers. They would go on to play a major role in Cody's life and begin the love and development of his ability to play wheelchair sports.

Cody loved his teacher, and he began to charm people all over the school as well as all over the parish. The children seemed to accept him and began to help him. As we had feared, he was exposed to some words and ideas that, for us, were morally unacceptable. He even quoted a word occasionally from the graffiti on the boys' bathroom wall. The good news was that we had this very open relationship, and he told us everything. I explained to him he was going to read lots of things on lots of bathroom walls, and it would be better not to recite them to anyone. We laugh about that now.

Overall, kindergarten was great. He did learn to read and developed many other skills. That was the first year of Misty, Cody's first young love. He and Misty would wear us out with the telephone, love notes, etc., for the next seven years. The only real negative during that year was recess. Cody could not run, he was thrown from the merry-go-round on the second day (making all of us scared of it), he could not stand up to play foursquare, and he couldn't handle the monkey bars. Therefore, recess was bad for him. He sat alone on a bench most of the time, and every once in a while a child would come over and talk to him. Of course, battery operated riding toys were not allowed. I bought a $1200 bike to ride with his hands, but because his feet had to be strapped on the pedals to ride, he hated it. Most problems had a solution, no matter how difficult, and we could eventually conquer them, but we just couldn't seem to fix recess. He crawled a lot at home to play football, etc., but even with kneepads at school, he would wind up getting hurt. If we were ever available during recess time, Paul or I would go by to distract him. However, when I would drive up and see him sitting alone on that bench watching the other kids run and play, it would tear my heart out. He eventually learned to get a chair and play foursquare, but we still never really fixed recess. Years later, wheelchair sports would do that for him.

Kindergarten graduation was adorable. We put a chair on the stage and helped him to get up there, and he played a song on his violin for the talent show. That school year was great, but unknown to us, there was a storm coming that had been brewing all his life. The eye of that storm had formed so slowly it blindsided us, and the whole experience took its toll on the entire family.

I suppose most people's lives are somewhat of a roller coaster ride, but raising a child with a disability has been like riding a 90-foot wave and crashing under it continuously. Prayer, family, and friends have kept us from drowning.

The summer Cody turned six we had a lot of great family time. We took a vacation to the Smoky Mountains, and we had a lot of fun just in our own back yard. Cody had become an excellent swimmer, so we would have the best time grilling food and eating out on the patio, while watching him swim. He seemed healthy, though he was always pale and thin. I thought it was because we used sunscreen and he never ate much, but he talked so well and was ordinarily in a good mood. He kept all of us entertained. What we had failed to notice for some reason (probably a combination of his wonderful personality and our denial) was how much his head had grown. That's why, when we decided to do his six-month check up with the neurosurgeon the week before he started first grade, I was willing to take him there by myself. On the way, we sang, laughed, and told jokes. He seemed healthy to me. We sat in the waiting room our usual one and a half hours and Cody entertained everyone there. When they called Cody to the back, the doctor measured his head and then sent him to a separate building behind his office to do CT scans of his head. That routine was normal on our visits there so I was not alarmed. The guy doing the scans knew us well, but he was also well trained not to reveal any abnormalities he identified. Dr. J. was very adamant that all reports be given only to a child's parents and only by him. So we saw no unusual reaction to the films.

Therefore, we anxiously awaited the doctor's report only because we were ready to leave. When he entered the exam room the second time, films in hand, we were laughing and joking. He put the films on the view-box, turned on the light, and a look of despair came across his face. His talk began with, "Momma, I do not want you to get upset, but I have some very bad news." That old familiar lump rose in my throat.

My words were, "Oh no, what is it?"

He continued. "You know the baby's head has continued to grow above the normal curve. The fluid in the ventricles, I believe, has reached a very dangerous level. and we need to insert a tube to drain that fluid, a tube called a ventricular/peritoneal shunt. The surgery is done all the time on these children. Most have them from birth. He was lucky to go this long without one, but I believe if the fluid continues to increase, the pressure will become very dangerous for him."

It was one of those moments that would sneak up on you and body slam you like a professional wrestler. I cried out, "Oh, my God. I thought after six years that we had won that battle. I don't want to put him in that kind of danger. What will happen if we decide not to do it?" My tears were flowing like a rain shower.

He carefully explained in a tone much more kind than usual, "He needs to have it done. The danger of not doing it is much greater than doing the surgery. If the pressure becomes too great, he will lose his sight. I can still put the shunt in and relieve the pressure, but the blindness would be permanent."

My thoughts ran wild, but the foremost one was, *Again, we are going to be forced to pick from a group of bad choices.* My next question was, "How is the surgery done?"

I still don't know the details because his first sentence was, "You shave his head bald and drill two small holes in the side of his skull . . .," and he lost me after that.

Most people cannot even imagine discussing drilling holes in their baby's head, now we would have to allow it to be done. I was horrified, but when I looked at the panic in Cody's eyes, I knew I needed to calm down and think of him. For the next 20 minutes, I worked at getting Dr. J. to find an alternate, safe plan. Anything but what he had just described. There just wasn't one. In my mind, I can still see Dr. J. holding his head in his hands, shaking it and saying, "Oh Jesus, help me Jesus." We were both overwhelmed, me at the thought of the surgery and the danger it brought, and him with trying to deal with the hysterical mother I had become when he delivered his bad news. He also dropped the bomb on me that it had already become a risky situation, and he wanted to admit him to the hospital in three days. No warning, no time to brace yourself, just head straight into the storm with your precious child's life at stake. We were the last people in his office before lunch, and I believe he took the afternoon off to recover from our visit. I didn't have that luxury. Like all the terrible circumstances spina bifida created in our lives, there was nowhere to turn, nowhere to hide, nowhere to run to but the Cross. There is a song that consists of these words:

> *I must tell Jesus all of my troubles.*
> *I cannot bear these burdens alone;*
> *In my despair He kindly will help me,*
> *He ever loves and cares for His own.*[13]

That song played repeatedly in my head as I drove home. Bless Cody's heart. He had sat there so bravely while we debated the shunt issue. He watched his mother turn hysterical and his doctor pound into her the necessity of the danger. It must have been terrifying for a six-year-old. I heard evidence of that when he began to fire questions at me, "Will I feel the drill on my head? Will my hair ever grow back? Will I die? Does this mean we can't go to the beach? Will it make me fail first grade to miss that much?" I felt sick. I comforted him as much as I could, even though I was distraught myself. Most little boys at six years old were out hitting a baseball or riding their bikes or a horse, fishing, watching TV, playing videos, or camping out with their friends. Mine was dreading a doctor drilling into his head. I know God has a master plan. Sometimes it is just hard to figure it out. That was one of those times.

Dropping that bomb on the other people who loved Cody was atrocious, yet necessary. As always, the next day was a Friday, and we would have to live through a nightmare weekend. On top of that, we had planned an end-of-summer weekend to the beach in Florida. We decided it would not be fair to Cody to cancel it. What if things didn't go well with the surgery? We acted as if the surgery were a long time off so he could enjoy the trip. The rest of us, Paul, Ma, and I felt like we were on the beach awaiting our doom. I have experienced better trips to Florida, for sure, but Cody had a blast. For hours Paul and Cody rode the waves on a raft, and Cody laughed every time they spilled into the ocean. Ma and I sat on the beach and cried. Cody slept as we drove home, and the rest of us rode in silence, absorbed in our thoughts and prayers.

On Monday morning, we arrived at the hospital very early. They drew Cody's blood, took x-rays, got a urine sample, and started an IV. We were exhausted in the first two hours. The surgery was slated for the next morning. The calls and appearances of the "angels among us" were many. That was so much help because it kept Cody talking and laughing. That night, however, fear and dread surrounded us. I took his little hand and we prayed. I assured him God would send angels to watch over him in surgery because I couldn't. None of us slept that night.

They came very early the next morning to take him back to the holding room and shave his head. The person who came to get Cody was a friend of mine, Bob, the huge guy who was Dr. J.'s nurse. He told Cody he was going to shave his head and be his bodyguard. Cody smiled. I'm sure not many people thought of that huge man as an angel, but we sure did. We followed them to the door of surgery. Cody was dressed in a tiny gown and wearing a giant paper cap. We gave him a kiss and told him we loved him and promised to be there when he woke up. He said, "I'm scared, Mom."

I choked out, "I know, Son, but God will take care of you. Bob and Dr. J. will be there too."

He replied reluctantly, "Okay." When they disappeared behind the surgery door with my brave little boy on his way to what I perceived to be the greatest danger of his very short but difficult life, I felt like falling to my knees. My chest hurt, breathing was difficult, and my tears turned to sobs. Our friends and family surrounded us in support, but the most awful moment was yet to come. Just as I was about to try to find a seat to wait out the surgery, Paul took my hand and whisked me down the hall away from the others. He said in his most frightened voice ever, "I don't want them to do the surgery. I have a really bad feeling about it. I'm afraid he will die. Let's tear up the consents and take him home. Please, please. Don't let them kill our baby." Every time I thought we had reached the lowest point, another blow would come.

I knew how much he loved that child, and it was a most terrible moment. I reached for what courage I had left and I declared, "Paul, I am scared too. I just keep remembering his threat of blindness if the pressure becomes too great. As well as Cody does, we would be dealing with a completely new level of difficulty with blindness. Can you live with that, knowing we could have prevented it? I can't." He said, "Me neither, but I have a terrible feeling about the surgery. Maybe he won't go blind without it."

"And maybe he will."

He asked, "What can we do?"

My reply was, "Well, I don't think this morning is the time for a standoff." As we stood and cried, Dr. J. stormed in demanding, "What in the heck are y'all doing? The baby is ready to go in, and y'all are down here away from where I told you to be." Neither one of us said anything. We followed him back to the waiting area like two scolded puppies. He can be rough, but again, he does know how to diffuse a situation.

That two-hour wait seemed like it took months. I threw up twice. My nose bled. What if Paul's feeling was right? Would our child survive and continue to be the little boy we adored? It was up to God. It was in His hands.

We all survived, though it took its toll. Everyone there was tense. The mood was grim. Then at the point we could hardly bear it, they rolled Cody out on a stretcher, right through the middle of our group of supporters. His head was bandaged and he was pale, but he was awake with his stretcher raised in almost a sitting position. He actually smiled, waved his little hand to the family and our dear friends, and said, "Hey!" as if it were a normal gathering. I couldn't believe it.

I was so relieved that I cried aloud, "Thank you, Lord!" Little did we know the trial was not over.

Cody seemed to be doing well so it was a blow when they rolled him directly to the Pediatric Intensive Care Unit and left us on the outside of the locked, coded doors without the code. Most of our supporters left after giving us phone numbers and promises of checking on us later that day. Right away Dr. J. sent for Paul and me to come to a conference room inside the PICU. He reported how well the surgery went and said that the fluid ejected through the shunt with such a force when it was inserted that he felt going without it for any longer would have surely cost Cody his sight. We listened very intently, and without saying it, we both were thankful and pleased with the decision to consent to it, especially with the successful outcome. Dr. J. also made his speech we had heard many times about impending retardation, no normal life expectancy, etc. It was odd; that speech had always made us go limp before. This time I thought, *Oscar Mayer invented a word for that speech, which is B-O-L-O-G-N-A!* But I didn't say it. I had too much respect and admiration for Dr. J. I knew he felt he always had to prepare us for the worst. Instead, we thanked him for his skill and care of Cody and asked if we could go in. He said we could for a few minutes only. No one could have ever prepared us for what happened next. No one had even tried.

When Paul and I went into Cody's room, there was a very nice male nurse with him. He was bringing in a TV/VCR with children's tapes for Cody to watch. Paul sat in a chair on one side of the bed, and I was on the other side. Cody looked very pale, and he was staring straight ahead holding the nurse-call button in his right hand. I touched his hand and began to talk to him softly in case he had a headache. He made no response to anything I said. He didn't look at us or answer any of our questions. I pleaded with him to talk to us, to tell me what was driving the silence. Was it pain, fear, anger . . . what? The most shocking part of that visit followed. There was a pitcher of water and a cup on the table right beside the bed. As I continued to plead to no avail for Cody to talk to us, he pressed the button in his hand. When the nurse appeared, he asked him, "Can I have some water please?" My hand was two inches from that water. Paul and I felt like we were in the twilight zone.

I kept pleading with him, "Baby, are you mad at us? Are you scared? Are you upset because we can't stay with you? Please tell Momma and Daddy what is wrong."

He still said nothing. After a few minutes, the staff said we had to leave. We kissed him, told him we loved him, and we would be camped right outside the door. He remained silent and so did Paul. I felt ill. Once outside the unit, I fell apart. Paul sat with me and cried. We were so puzzled about his silence, and we were so frightened. We prayed that nothing was hidden that we weren't aware of.

I knew Paul wanted a break, so I sent him to get food. The hospital is surrounded by fast food places, so I knew he would not go far. Right after he left, the nurse came to the door and told me Cody was throwing up. She had called Dr. R., Cody's pediatrician, and he was on his way. He came by me on his way in and said as soon as he took care of him he would come and let me know what was going on. I was so thankful. I was terrified and Paul was still gone. So many people had been there during the surgery that there had not been enough places to sit. Now I was all alone. It seemed like hours went by, and Dr. R. did not come out. Finally, I was so frightened I knocked on the PICU door. When the nurse looked out and saw it was just me, he let me in. I rushed into Cody's cubicle and found Dr. R. lying beside Cody in the bed playing an electronic game on a handheld Game Boy system. I exclaimed, frightened and irritated, "Why are you in here playing Game Boy when I am outside that door scared to death?"

He replied with a smile, "Cody quit vomiting as soon as he saw me, and I have never played this game before." Our little monkey had a clown for a doctor. At least Cody was okay. Two days later that same doctor would have the college athletic department's secretary to stop football practice and tell two of Cody's favorite players to come to the PICU and bring Cody a football and a jersey. Dr. R. really loves kids and they love him. That makes illnesses so much more bearable.

It took four miserable days in PICU before Cody stopped throwing up for good and kept food down. Every time Dr. J. came, he and I would argue. He would tell me we should go to the movie and relax; let the nurses take care of Cody. I would tell him we would be right outside the door. I know he just wanted us to relieve our stress, but I am just not made that way. I had to be where my sick child was, even if he refused to talk to me.

When the four days had passed, they moved us to a room on the Pediatric Unit. Dr. J. still would not let anyone in that room with Cody but Paul and me. Paul went back to work, and Cody and I stayed there for nine long days and nights. The surgery had been a great success. No more silent treatment, and even now when I ask Cody about that he can't explain it. He just says he had to "zone out" to tolerate the pain. I left that alone. All I know is that he hardly slept any those nine days because he felt so good. The relief of pressure in his head had done wonders for him. He was like a caged animal, and he did things like calling the desk and telling the nurses I had been abducted by aliens so when I emerged from the shower across the hall I found the room full of nurses, supervisors, and security. When they looked astonished to see me walk in, he told them, "Sorry, guys. I was just lonesome." Thank goodness they loved him so they took it well. On another night, I came out of the bathroom and twenty minutes later the pizza man knocked at the door and delivered two large pizzas that little Mr. Monkey had ordered.

When we finally got discharged, I left there thanking God we had the shunt surgery done in time to save his sight, at the same time praying that I would not be closed up in a room with that child for nine days, see a bullet-pop Popsicle, or hear the theme song from N-N-N-Nick-at-Nite again as long as I lived.

Cody's recovery was smooth and rapid. I had long since learned how to help him rebuild his strength and heal his scars. We had never seen him thrive so well before. It became clear to all of us that the surgery had been truly necessary and beneficial. Within a week, he was typing away on the computer and asking about going out to ride his four-wheeler. We made him hold off on riding it until we were sure his incisions were well-knitted. When we returned to Dr. J.'s office four weeks after the surgery, he told us Cody could return to school. I asked him for an excuse for Cody because he had missed the first month of school. He exploded, "No. Darn bureaucracy! They should believe you!

Tell them to call my office if they need an excuse, and I will give them one!" I know he was defending me, but I did not want any confrontation with the school, any more than was necessary, since we already had the task of breaking in a new crew to the braces, crutches, etc., and catching up on what he had missed the first month. So I went to the pediatrician and got the excuse. Nothing was ever easy.

When I went to the school to arrange for Cody's return, there was good news and bad news. The good news was that I knew his teacher. I had been friends with her family and gone to church with them for years and knowing that was a great relief. The bad news came during the IEP meeting when the physical therapist said, "We are not going to be able to let him stay in regular classes because his feet won't touch the floor in a regular desk. We need to put him in special education classes where we have the right equipment." The rest of the group sat in silence waiting for my response. I may have seemed weak and reserved to them because I was going through my crash-and-burn period that comes after each crisis, but I rose to the occasion. I challenged all of them, "Y'all are kidding, right? You have each bumped your head somewhere if you think my child is going to be put in special education for that reason. Do you have a maintenance man?" They all seemed stupefied by that question. Therefore, I repeated it. "Do you have a maintenance man for this school?" (I knew full well that was a requirement.)

Finally, the principal admitted, "We have Mr. Charley."

I came back with, "Go get Mr. Charley." They sent for him immediately. They knew I was mad. Mr. Charley arrived and it was easy to see he was very intimidated. I did not hesitate, because I knew he wanted to be released from that meeting as soon as possible. I asked him, "Mr. Charley, could you build a small square platform about three inches high that would clamp to the front of Cody's desk so he could put his feet on it?"

Mr. Charley did not hesitate but replied, "Oh, yes, ma'am. No problem. I will have that ready for him in two days and will bring it to Ms. K.'s room and install it."

My heartfelt words were, "Thank you. You are a nice and helpful man, and Cody will be indebted to you, sir." Mr. Charley left, beaming, and set out to accomplish his task.

I looked harshly at the rest of that group and scolded, "How easy was that? Mr. Charley takes more pride in his work than most people do. Anyone who forces a bright child to stay in class with mentally challenged kids because of a necessary simple alteration to the physical setting of a room should be ashamed. If Cody were mentally challenged, we would accept that and set our course appropriately, but he is not. Also, the fact that the P.T., the very person who should be helping him to reach his full potential, is the one who suggested that is shocking. Please make sure he is taken care of. Call me if there are any problems. Here is a list of the goals he should be able to accomplish. Put them with yours and I will sign the paper work. Cody will be here for regular class the day after tomorrow. This meeting is over."

Sobbing, I practically ran to the car. No one else I knew had to go through that kind of battle before her child could start first grade. We had already lived through the horror of the shunt. I was so angry. I went to the store and bought a bottle of water, drank it, and calmed down before I returned home. The only things I told Cody were that he had a sweet teacher and that Mr. Charley was going to build him a platform to put his feet on. I told Cody to be sure and thank Mr. Charley. Cody was so excited about school, and he had enough obstacles facing him, so I never told him of the entire conversation.

As we prepared for his first day back at school, I was concerned. Concerned about the teacher being able to lock and unlock the contraption braces he was wearing then, about his catching up on his work after missing a whole month, but most of all about what reaction the kids would have to his shaved head and that shunt sitting there under the skin like a water hose. I talked to Cody briefly the first morning back and told him the kids would be naturally curious, and I thought the best course was to talk about it as little as possible, then change the subject. He said he was okay with that. When we started down the hall of the school, the first person we met was Mr. Charley. He said, "I just wanted you to know the platform is built and clamped to his desk." Cody and I thanked him and let him know he was a hero to us. Mr. Charley was so proud. He would greet us on the first day of school for the next two years to let us know he had moved the platform and clamped it to Cody's assigned desk for that year. After that, Cody could rest his feet on the floor comfortably without it. Nobody really expected a maintenance man to be an angel, but in our experience, Mr. Charley was just that.

We ventured on to Cody's class and checked out the platform, which was perfect. We had arrived early to fill out forms and show the teacher how to handle the braces. Honestly, even for us the braces were atrocious to deal with. She seemed skeptical, but determined. As the other children began to arrive, they stared in amazement at Cody's braces, but they seemed very happy to see him. I wanted to go and let Cody work things out for himself. I cried as I drove to work. It would be something I would do the first school day of every year. The fears and concerns were overwhelming. All day I cried off and on. I was so anxious to pick him up that afternoon to smooth over any hurt feelings he had from comments by the kids that day. (I learned then that predicting reactions, even of kids, is almost impossible. When or if you can understand that, you can save yourself a lot of unnecessary worry.)

When it was nearing time for school to dismiss his first day back, I rushed to the school to pick him up. I very much wanted to be there to comfort him about the blows I thought he would surely have taken that day and put an end to that most miserable day. When I arrived and parked at the school, the first thing that met my eyes was Cody coming out surrounded by little girls carrying his books and supplies while his book bag remained strapped on his back, empty. They were all laughing and he was glowing with excitement. I knew right away I had wasted another day of despair while he was thriving. I was exhausted but greatly relieved.

When he got in the car and all the little girls spoke to me and said flirty good-byes to him, my first question was, "How was your day?"

His reply was, "Super." He began to tell me how the other children had been delighted and excited to see him back, about all of the activities they had planned, and as usual, he had a sarcastic note for me about coming up to speed on his work. That remark was, "Gee, Mom, I don't know why you were worried about me catching up on my work. Those goofballs hadn't been doing nuttin' but reviewing stuff we did in kindergarten, and they don't seem like they know it any better than they did then."

I smothered a laugh but still had some lingering concerns about staring, etc., so I asked, "Hey, Pal, did anything unusual happen today?"

My heart fell to my feet when he replied, "Well, as a matter of fact it did." I inquired, "Well, do you want to tell your old mom?"

He chuckled and I was puzzled. After a minute he just blurted out, "Misty was there and she whispered to me that she wanted to sex me."

Well, howdy doody. After I caught my breath I gasped out, "What did you tell her?"

He chuckled again and replied, "I told her I wanted to sex her too. But Mom, there is a slight problem."

I said emphatically, "There certainly is, Son."

Before I could go on, he interrupted loudly with, "What is sex?"

Needless to say, I was relieved that he had not been given details by anyone. My answer was, "Not anything 6-year-olds need to be involved with. You tell Miss Misty to do her schoolwork and behave and you do the same. When you are old enough, Daddy will explain."

In his usual trusting way he said, "Okay, Mom." This time I believe he was the one relieved. He had an idea he was out of his boundaries.

I added, "By the way, Pal, don't tell people you want to do things if you don't know what they are."

He replied with a nod, "Good idea, Mom."

Well, there you go. I had wasted a whole night and day fretting and crying believing he would be made fun of because of his baldness and shunt, and all the while, he is being taught obscene ideas by his illustrious six-year-old girlfriend. Boy, there was always a surprise around every corner!

After the first day, with redesigning the IEP and the teacher conquering the locking and unlocking of the braces, Cody adjusted well to first grade. The rest of the year went by smoothly. That year was our first introduction to having an adaptive physical education teacher. He came every day and worked with Cody for an hour in the gym. He let him cast a rod and reel, shoot basketball, etc. We never fixed recess, but that helped to relieve his despair over it. That was really his first introduction to sports, other than with his dad, and we had no idea that sports activities would play such a vital part in his life for many years.

One day Cody came home extremely excited, waving a sign up

form for Dixie Youth baseball. I was astonished that they had given him that form without discussing it with us first. I gently tried to caution him that there might be some problems with playing in a regular league. When we went to the Saturday sign up, two of the guys at the table, buffed-up jocks, the type who want to appear to be God's gift to sports, snubbed us completely and said they knew no way to help us, but the other guy gave me the name of a coach who might help. I didn't let Cody see the hurt, but it was one of many times we would be treated like second-class citizens because of the handicap, even after I said we knew there would be problems. We did not want to make things difficult or uncomfortable for anyone; Cody just wanted to play ball.

I wanted to run from the whole idea to protect Cody from rejection and disappointment. Thank goodness, I did not do that. It would be the first of many stepping-stones to Cody's later great successes in sports and his ability to inspire others. I just kept thinking, *No matter how much it hurts, there is a reason God made him this way, and I know He wants us to face adversity head on.* So I prayed, *Lord, let this coach be an 'angel among us' and help us. Cody wants to play ball so badly, and I believe you want him to. Help us to persevere and find a way.*

When I finished praying, I took a deep breath and dialed the number. One of the kindest voices I had ever heard came on the other end of the line and identified himself as Coach Mike. He, too, would be considered by most of his peers to be an unlikely "angel among us," but he would become exactly that in Cody's life.

The season was fall ball, and the way the coach worked things out was for Cody to sit in a chair to bat and then put a runner in for him. He got some really good hits. When the team was in the outfield, he played catcher with a boy behind him to retrieve balls that got away from him. Not many got away, and the other boys, while disgusted and impatient with him at first, little by little, gained respect and learned to love Cody. That was a really neat experience. Cody loved the dugout as much as anything else, probably because that was a place where he was equal to the others. He could just be one of the guys and forget about the spina bifida for a moment. It wasn't easy, but Cody was thrilled. The pictures in his uniform were of great worth to us.

At the end of the season, the coach made it a point to meet with us. He looked sad when he reported, "Cody is a great kid, and he has been a real inspiration to me, to all of us, but I am afraid he will not be able to get on a team in the spring when things are more serious."

I replied, "Paul and I have already realized that some of these little league parents are out for blood. I suppose most have visions of these six-year-old boys going pro some day. That is not our goal. We are going to move on to the challenger league, but we thank you for this wonderful opportunity for one very dedicated little boy. He will always love Coach Mike and so will we." We had a tearful departure.

We did move on to the challenger league, where kids with disabilities got a chance to play baseball under the coaching of some men who had a heart full of love for them and who also knew how to coach baseball. It was amazing; every one of those men could have coached in the regular leagues but chose that one, including Paul who had been an excellent baseball player when he was younger. He became a coach in that league for the next ten years. Every spring we drove 100 miles each way every Saturday for eight weeks to play. They had a tennis court surface baseball diamond so the wheelchairs would not be in the mud. Cody hit a lot of grand slams. When a team formed in our town, Cody and Paul suggested to their team that we might do well not to drive that far. Well, by golly, the mothers started to cry about the possibility of losing Coach Paul. Needless to say, we stayed with them until Cody was too old to play. It was definitely quality time for father, son, and the whole family. Sometimes friends like Dot, who was like a grandmother to Cody, and Traci, who had helped us through a crisis, made the trip to the ball park with us, and each one of them would say what a blessing it was to see it.

The only sad thing came at the first game of each season. It seemed there was always a child who had passed away between seasons, and each season began with the mother or father of that child throwing in the first pitch, after that child's coach had given an "in memory" speech. We would all cry, but it reminded us that our lives are brief and that we all live on in the memories of others. I told Cody that while it made us sad, it emphasized more than anything else that we should make every day count and do everything we could to help others. He agreed.

One day in late summer I was washing clothes, and Cody was watching TV in the den. I emerged from the laundry room, and he was missing. I looked in his room, but he was not there. I called him—no answer. I then went outside and saw his crutches at the bottom of this 40-foot tree. I looked up, and there he was perched on a limb halfway up that tree. I couldn't believe it! He smiled and coolly said, "Hi, Mom!"

As calmly as I could, I instructed him, "I don't know how you got up there, but you get down the same way, and I will see you in the house shortly." I went inside. I was too scared to watch.

I was about to get a ladder or call 911 when here he came snapping those crutches as loudly as he could and shouting, "The first time in my life I get to climb a tree, and you make me get down!"

"Sorry, but we have spent a million dollars repairing those hips, and I don't like head injuries." Later on, we laughed about it.

The summer that Cody turned seven, he was as happy and healthy as he had ever been. We had many fun family outings that summer—picnics, fishing trips, and grilling out by Ma's pool. Meanwhile, Cody was growing into some kind of character.

In the second week of August, things seemed to be shaping up to be a normal school year. Paul and Cody were bracing themselves for school to start. By that time, Paul had gone back to college and gotten a second degree—this time in education. We had grown so weary of rejection from places that provided childcare that we decided never to face that hurdle again. Paul became a teacher, and that way he was off work when Cody was out of school. They were able to spend the summers creating many wonderful father/son adventures. Paul taught him to accomplish every sport known to man—in spite of his disability. What a dad!

On that morning in the middle of August, I left for work with the two of them sound asleep, as usual. Even though there were some "honey do" jobs that I wanted Paul to do before school started, he would soon be leaving home at 6:30 A.M. five days a week, so I decided to leave them at peace. There was only one week left for them to sleep late. It is so odd how life-changing days seem to always start out so peacefully. On the way to work that morning, I thought about how, despite all of the challenges and turmoil since Cody's birth, we still managed to have some semblance of normal family life—at least normal for us. I thanked God for His love and our love for each other. I prayed for peace and guidance, and for some reason, I felt led to pray that He would brace us for upcoming changes that were to come to our lives. That day would bring an event that would change all of our lives forever. I didn't know it; I couldn't see it coming, but it would.

Looking back now, the whole memory of that time reemphasized something I tell Cody often, "God has a plan and we don't know what it is. We don't even know what it is for five minutes from now, so we should always keep our lives as straight and as simple as possible. That way whatever storms come our way, we are ready." Ready or not, this storm blew into our lives, and with it came one of the biggest blessings we could ever have received.

When I arrived at the hospital that morning the staff was waiting anxiously for me. They repeated to me a saying I use on them to this day, "Empty your bladder, put on your roller skates, and get ready to rock and roll." That means a lot of challenging deliveries are about to occur. Before that eight-hour shift was done, fifteen new lives would have entered the world, and one of them would embrace my family as we embraced her.

In the middle of all of the confusion of that afternoon, two of the nurses from the OB unit appeared at the nurses' station of the NICU wanting to talk to me. Being mentor, friend, and helper to everyone, I was not alarmed, but I was also in no way expecting the news they had brought. This is what they said, "There is a lady who came into the labor unit saying she was having a miscarriage. Instead, she just delivered a beautiful 7 pound 10 ounce baby girl. She is very, very verbal about putting her up for adoption. She is not from this area and has no arrangements made. This would be a perfect child for you and Paul. Plus, we called social services and they are gone for the day. All you have to do is get her to sign the baby over to your attorney."

Now many times situations arise where you are not sure of the course you should take. This was not one of them. God had dropped this most wonderful bundle in our laps, and from that moment on, I knew it would work out. She had blindsided us. We had talked about adoption but never pursued it, and we didn't really have a specific attorney, but we knew some attorneys. I just knew in my heart, from the moment they rolled that little doll baby past me in that isolette, adopting her was the right thing and that she would be bossing us around for at least the next 21 years.

As soon as my nurses saw her, they got so excited and started hounding me, "Call Paul! Call Paul!" I took a deep breath and did just that. I couldn't help but wonder, as I punched those numbers, if Paul had any idea what vast territory "for better or worse, for richer or poorer, in sickness and in health" really covered. When he answered the phone, I could hear several children in the background. Considering the time constraints with the pending closure of the lawyer's offices, I jumped right into it.

After I explained the situation, he obviously thought I was joking because his reply was, "Why don't we adopt our neighbor's kids? I have been trying to get them to go home for two hours!" Then I heard a calamity in the background and he said, "Let me go," and hung up.

I was in shock. The nurses demanded in unison, "What did he say? What did he say?"

I reported, "I don't believe he thought I was serious. We'll call him back in a minute." Before I could dial the number, the phone rang and it was Paul.

"Are you serious?" he asked.

My answer was, "Yes, and we only have fifteen minutes to decide."

He gave his consent with, "Go ahead and call the lawyer, but you are the craziest woman I have ever known in my life. Who goes to work and comes home with a new child?"

I came back with, "Hopefully, I do."

His only other concern for the moment was, "Is she healthy?"

"As far as I can tell she is, and she is adorable. She has lots of dark curly hair and is very alert. Paul, I know this is a risk, but it feels so right. I tell you this, she doesn't have Down's syndrome or spina bifida, and at my age and with our history, those are two guarantees we could not get if we had another baby. Plus, she is full-term and no resuscitation was required. That's all we can know. There is no time to obtain any other background information."

Hesitantly, he said, "Go on, call S.J., and let me know what he says."

"Are you okay with this? Because, it is your life too."

"I am. I'm just not used to taking big risks like you are, but like everything else in our lives, I am willing to trust you and God to handle it."

"I love you! We have a daughter! Can you believe it? Let me go so I can call S.J. before he leaves." I knew the storm had taken him by total surprise just as it had me.

When I called S.J., he told me he would quickly prepare the proper surrender papers and bring them to the hospital that night for the birth mother to sign. He added, "Some day you are going to call me during normal business hours with a normal request." I knew that wouldn't happen. We had dropped the word "normal" from our vocabulary over seven years before that.

What he had told me to do was to go to the recovery room where the lady was, be sure she wanted to go through with the adoption process, and have her call him from there. By this time, I was shaking all over. I removed my name badge and went in to see her. I told her that my husband and I would love to adopt her baby if she would allow us the privilege of doing so. This was her reply, "I don't want you to think I am a wild woman off the street. I have been to college; I just can't handle raising a child. I want you to know I saw the baby Jessica story on TV, and I would never do that to anyone. If I am mature enough to put her up for adoption, I am mature enough to leave y'all alone and let you raise her."

I wasn't sure what to say, but this is what came out, "If it means anything, she will be well loved and well cared for."

She replied, "All of those people in blue and all of those people in pink already told me that." I just grinned.

"Well, we only have a short period of time this afternoon to arrange things. I would like for you to talk to my attorney on the phone, and then tonight he will bring the papers for you to sign." She looked startled and that caused me to be alarmed.

"They are going to let me go in an hour."

"You mean to a room right?"

She said, "No, home to my friend's house." I was really scared then, as I tried to reason with her.

I told her, "That is too dangerous. You should stay here where the nurses can take care of you."

Her response was, "If I have any bleeding or problems I will come back to the emergency room, but I have to go. It is just too depressing any other way. I will go to the lawyer's office in the morning and sign whatever papers I need to, I promise." I felt sick. *What if she changed her mind? What if she deserted her and child protection became part of the equation?* Again, we would just have to step out on faith. Again, God would show up. I also had the feeling this was the first of many obstacles along the road to finalizing an adoption. That turned out to be a real understatement.

We rolled her stretcher to the phone, and she made an arrangement with our attorney to do paperwork in his office early the next morning. I had a whole evening ahead of me to pray that she would keep her part of that arrangement. Little did I know that would not be the only prayer on my list. Before bedtime, I would have to help Paul and Ma both to have an attitude adjustment about adopting that baby.

Just as she had said she would, the birth mother left one hour after delivery. I couldn't help but think how strange it was for her to pop into my life and hand us a baby, then leave with the possibility of never seeing her again. Life does take some strange turns. It is also weird how your views on life's issues and your prejudices change depending on where you are standing. I had thought before that giving a baby up for adoption was a horrible neglect. Now I realized that it was the ultimate sacrifice. Love comes packaged in many different ways, and miracles are sometimes hard to recognize. I am so thankful she entrusted us with the little miracle she left behind.

I went to the nursery, held the baby, and the entire nursery staff cried with me. We shared mixed emotions of amazement, celebration of life, and fear. After I held her for ten minutes, we were truly bonded, and as if lightening struck, I suddenly realized, *I have a baby. No plans, no warning, no clothes, no baby bed . . . My Lord, I better get going.* After a sweet kiss on her cheek, I put her back in the isolette and gave them explicit instructions for her care. (They rolled their eyes since I had well trained them in newborn care many years before.) Then I headed home with my head reeling with all sorts of thoughts and plans. One thing that hit me was how odd some aspects of life were. Bonding with Cody had presented a frustration because he was sick and hooked to machines and taking care of sick babies all those years in the NICU made it seem weird that I had a sick baby. This little baby, not planned, not born of me, had dropped from Heaven with no warning, and I bonded with her immediately. Hard to figure, but not as much as the scene that met me when I arrived home.

I expected Paul and Ma to be looking for baby things in the attic, to be excited, making lists of needed supplies, making lots of phone calls, breaking Cody into the idea of a baby sister, anything but what I found. They were sitting at the dining room table with a large box of tissues between them, crying. Both of them, crying. I demanded, "What in the world are y'all crying about?" I could tell they were not tears of joy.

The response was, "We are afraid, afraid Cody won't get everything he needs if we take on another child. Afraid we can't ever love another child the way we do him."

The expression "Blow me down!" fit that moment. I cut into them. My words were, "What is wrong with y'all? Are y'all crazy? Do you actually think any one of us would shut down on Cody when he is only seven years old? If I thought for one second that I could not do everything I need to for him *and* her, I would never even consider this adoption! Besides, one of the main reasons I want to do this is for him, so he will have a little sister. Now dry up the tears. We have to make this place ready for a new baby!" That was the end of the crying that day.

Some of the baby things in the attic could be cleaned up and used, but after seven years in storage, some could not. The medical expenses in those days prevented savings, and we hadn't exactly planned for the coming of a new child. Just as I sat pondering how to manage, several of my nurses, friends I had worked with for years, young women with small children, started showing up. Before bedtime, we had everything we needed for the first year. What a blessing! News had spread like wildfire, and I prayed it would all work out well. It did.

The next morning I woke up at 4 A.M., got dressed, and went to work. I believe there were two reasons for that: One was I knew that way it would be real and not like the dream I often had of Cody running to me in a field and then awaken to find out it was not real. The other reason was my desire and commitment to bond with the baby. When I arrived, several "near retirement" L.P.N.'s were on duty. They had her dressed like a doll in a pink drawstring gown with lace and ruffles and a pink bow in her hair. Outfits surrounded her crib, and balloons were tied on the frame. One of the ladies said to me, "Why are you here? We are having so much fun playing with our grandbaby." My heart was full. It is wonderful to have such strong ties with the people you work with. They actually had a rocker ready in the corner because they knew I would be there early and that I would want a private moment with my new daughter. Those ladies have all retired now, and one has died. I miss them and their caring ways a lot. We all followed the rules (most of the time anyway), and we absolutely took good care of the babies in our charge. (That's in the records.) Yet we also loved and cared about one another. That makes life's difficult times so much more tolerable and happy times so much more enjoyable. Thank God they were on my staff then!

When I sat in that rocker in the wee hours of that morning, rocking and loving on that precious child, I was deeply moved. I knew in those moments that a decision made in fifteen minutes time had brought one of the greatest blessings of our lives. I was right. Many people said we were crazy. They were also right.

That morning I made some important decisions. One was that she would not go home with me, with us, until the surrender papers were legal. That would be five days after they were signed. Although that was an extremely difficult decision, especially since I planned to start maternity leave that day, I knew it was right. I looked around that room filled with infants in cribs with their pink and blue paper shirts on, covered with hospital-issued blankets, compared to our baby in her beautiful clothes with a gorgeous white blanket, crocheted by one of the nurses, and I knew she would be safe and well cared for. The thing I also knew, and the reason for my decision, was that if I had attached so strongly to her in five minutes time, my family would do the same thing. I was not about to take a chance on taking her home, having Cody in awe of his new baby sister, and then the birth mother changing her mind. I knew she had told me the day before that would never happen, but sometimes what people say and what they do are two different things. I didn't know her. Oddly enough, I didn't want to know her. I didn't want to feel sorry for her or feel like we were taking her baby away from her. I believed she was an angel in our lives, sent to leave this wonderful child with us and move on.

Even so, I believe God expects you to use your common sense

and always guard the well-being of your family. I had learned the hard way that while He always answers prayers, He sometimes answers them, "NO." If that had happened, it would not have been the first time an event in my life would appear to be cruel and without purpose. I wasn't willing to expose Cody or the rest of the family to any unnecessary cruelty. She would have to stay the five days. I dreaded living through the wait, but I was used to waiting, stepping out on faith, and making difficult decisions. I was firm about that one.

On the other hand, I also decided that morning that I would do everything in my power to ensure the adoption went through. I believed God surprised us with that baby, and when that happens, you just have to go with it or you miss life's richest blessings. I didn't want that. I had accepted that spina bifida, as hard as it is to deal with, was our lot in life, and we were trying our best to make good on it. Be that as it may, I wanted all of us, especially Cody, to capture all the good things of life that we could as we went along our most challenging journey. This baby was one of the good things. Never mind the crisis of it. Yes, babies are a crisis. When they come, your life is changed forever. Changed wonderfully, but changed. Everything we thought and did would be changed by the addition of this precious little being to our family, but it was a change we needed. We couldn't exactly see that at the time, but that didn't matter because God sees our needs all the time. That's why He sent her.

That morning turned out to be an adventure in itself. When eight o'clock came, I went to see the Director of Nurses. She had been in that job for one week and did not know me well. I decided to have some fun with her. I went into her office and announced with a grin that I needed to take maternity leave. She said, trying not to be obvious about looking at my belly, "Congratulations! When do you need to start your leave?"

My stone-faced reply was, "Today." She went pale and was at a loss for words. Every once in a while, an OB patient would come to our hospital to be checked, go to the bathroom, and deliver a baby there. I believe she wondered that day if I had done that. I only let her ponder for a few minutes, searching her mind for the next, most appropriate question, before I gave her great relief by sharing the news, "We are adopting." She happily did the paper work for me. Over the next ten years, up to her retirement, we would become good friends. That morning certainly broke the ice.

With family leave papers in hand, I went back to the nursery to see the baby once more and give a brief job description and list of duties to the nurse who would take charge in my absence. Thank goodness she was a seasoned NICU nurse and supervisor. Even so, I assured her I was going nowhere but home to get ready and later take care of our new baby. She would be able to reach me by phone any time she needed to. Considering she had a one-day notice before taking charge, that was a great comfort to her.

When I arrived home that morning, Paul and Cody were pacing with anxiety. "Has S.J. called yet?" they asked in unison.

My reply was, "Calm down. Her appointment is not for another hour. By the way, once the papers are signed, the baby will remain at the hospital for five more days before we can bring her home." If their faces had been balloons that I had popped with a pin, they would not have deflated more. All that did was renew my determination to follow through with that decision. I hate deceit, but I knew their desire to have her home would cloud their judgment. As difficult as it was to endure their disappointment, I held firm. I knew giving her up would be much more difficult than waiting for her arrival. I handled that the best way I could. I led them to believe they had no choice. They didn't; I had taken charge and made that choice for all of us. Actually, that was not a gray area for me. Taking charge and making unpopular but healthy choices for Cody had been my job for seven years. All I did was add a new child to my list.

It was ten-thirty when S.J. called. We all three jumped when the phone rang. He had this news, "Raina, the people that come to your hospital to deliver never cease to amaze me. That woman showed up here this morning at 9:30 A.M. on the nose, looking like a million dollars, signed everything I presented to her, asked for nothing except for me to see that her child was well taken care of, waited for the court date with a promise to be there also, and left. I would never have suspected if I hadn't already known that she had a baby yesterday. God help us!"

"God help us indeed. What's next?"

He told me, "The surrender is not really legal for five days. However, she has legally signed custody over to me, so we can go pick her up now if y'all want to before I have to go to court, as long as the doctor writes discharge orders."

I believe he was very startled when I said, "No. Let's see . . . that means she can come home on Tuesday."

"Right." He knew the deal. He was just surprised, knowing my position at the hospital that I would choose to wait. It wasn't my position that bothered me. It was Cody's.

He went on to explain the next move was a court date where she, Paul, and I would all appear before a judge to formally petition the courts for the adoption process to take place. I told him that as far as we were concerned, the sooner the better. I thanked him for his help and hung up. When I relayed the information to the family, there was great celebrating. Ma and Cheryl were there also. I told Paul that I wanted to leave Cody in the den with them, and I wanted him to go in the hall with me. He obliged and immediately gave me a big hug and kiss. Men always think that way. Although I did want to celebrate one of the most joyous events of our marriage with him, what I really wanted was to ask him this, "What do you think about letting Cody pick out her name? I realize after being the only child for seven years, doted on by four adults, the competition of a little sister will be a challenge. I believe letting him name her will help them to form a special bond and cushion the bumps a little."

He reluctantly agreed. We went back into the den, and I told Cody to come sit on my lap. "Son, how would you like to pick out the baby's name? I have a book of names you can use as a guide and that would be something that would let her know how special she is to her big brother."

He was delighted. He said in his sweet little way, "It might take me a few days."

I answered, "You have five. What a wonderful boy you are to take on such a big, important job." He grinned, took the name book, and went straight to his room to begin his search for the perfect name. We secretly agreed that unless it was a monster name, we would go with it. It made Ma and Cheryl nervous. That turned out to be one of the worst ideas I ever had.

Two days later he called Paul and me into the den and made this announcement, "I have found the most beautiful name in the world."

He was beaming. Paul was silent. I took a deep breath, but not deep enough, and instructed him, "Go ahead, Son. Tell us what it is."

He was so cute and proud as he presented his choice. "Polyester-one word. Isn't that beautiful?" A wave of nausea passed across me.

Paul whispered in my ear, "I told you this was a bad idea." He was sure right about that. The best reply I could think of was, "All righty then. Let us think about it."

Cody immediately became upset and exclaimed loudly, "I knew it. Y'all don't like it. I knew you wouldn't really let me name her. Adults always say you can do big jobs and then don't let you."

I tried to console him, "It's not that Daddy and I don't want to keep our promise. It's just not the kind of name we were thinking of. Can we look at some other names with you?"

He came back with, "What for? Nobody likes what I like. Forget it." He went to his room and slammed the door. What a mess. Sometimes what starts out as an idea to bring the family closer together ends with a big confusion and hard feelings. I knew if I didn't come up with a decent recovery plan, this would be one of them.

Paul just sat there with that sarcastic grin and said, "Better think of something fast."

"I know, I know. I don't suppose we could consider . . . ?"

I didn't even need to finish before he replied, "Uh, I don't think any of us would be happy with her named after a fabric. Other people are already saying we are crazy. That would prove it. I think Cody would even grow up and ask why we didn't stop him. We should have just named her and let him help do something else."

Sarcastically, I remarked, "Easy to say that now, Mister." He laughed.

"Well, I better go talk to him. Start thinking of names. We only have three days to decide." I went into Cody's room, sat on his bed, and pleaded, "Baby, please don't think we don't value your opinion. It's just that whatever we name her we should all be happy with. It's what her name will be for the rest of her life. It will also be what we will always call her. Don't you think we should all like it?"

His very mature reply was, "Sure, Mom. Really, I think it should be the grown-ups' job to name babies. Let me do something else for her.

Okay? It's just too much pressure for a seven year old kid." I hugged him. At that moment, it seemed like his judgment was better than mine.

Years later one of his coaches would say to me, when I was asking about Cody's response to an assigned work out, "Raina, one thing I have learned about Cody. He may kick and scream about something, but in the end, he will always come back and do the right thing." I knew he was right because I had seen that in him that day. I made it okay by promising that he could hold her on the way home from the hospital, feed her the first bottle at home, be excused from changing dirty diapers, and when she was old enough, she could sometimes sleep on his top bunk. I remember thinking at times of much bigger crises, *I wish there was always an answer that readily available to solve Cody's problems.* Unfortunately, life just isn't always that simple.

There was also a name crisis concerning Paul. After it became our task to name the baby, he wanted to select Paula Kay, after some childhood sweetheart of his. My response to that was, "No way, Pal. You got in there the first time with Cody Paul. I am not having Cody Paul, Paula Kay, Pauline, Paulette. Forget it!" He chuckled and replied, "Okay then, my second choice is Nicole." My favorite was Abby, which he was hesitant about. We all finally agreed on Abby Nicole. Years later, in the midst of a fight, Cody would tell her, "Oh, shut up. If things had gone my way you would be named Polyester." The laughter broke up the fight. Obviously, he had come to appreciate our intervention on the name issue.

The day before Abby was coming to live with us, the whole family was excited. In a very late-night anxiety attack, I took Paul to see her. When we arrived at the nursery, viewing the sea of infants from the window, I asked, "Which one do you think she is?"

He pointed right to her and said, "I hope it's that one."

"That's her." He was hooked.

The name selection was not quite the only hurdle Cody needed to conquer before the arrival of the baby. The night before we were going to get her, I found him sitting on his bed deep in thought. My question to him was, "What are you thinking about, Son?"

He quickly responded, "Mom, I need to ask you something." I sat down in an effort to brace myself because he looked really worried. A harness could not have braced my heart enough to easily handle what

I heard. This is what he asked, "Mom, do you think the baby will like me even though I can't walk without braces and crutches?"

Through the tears, I offered these words of encouragement, "Son, I think she will love you. After all, you are her big, brave brother. Besides, who ever met you and didn't love you?" He smiled and seemed so relieved. Knowing he felt the disability might block her love for him broke my heart. Good thing I was too busy to dwell on it.

The morning of Abby's homecoming had finally arrived. The guidelines of releasing an infant to an attorney required us to meet him away from the hospital. I sent her pink, lacy outfit to the hospital with the lawyer's secretary. We were all so excited. I have survived many hard days by thinking back to that day and the expression on Cody's face when they placed that baby in his arms. We all cried. I have shared this thought with many audiences in presenting our story, "Maybe, just maybe, everything that was taken away from Cody was given back to all of us in Abby." On the way home, Cody held her and gave her a bottle. He kept kissing her on her head. She never whimpered. I believe his concerns about her liking him were gone for the moment, and she felt truly loved. Our family was so joyous on that most precious of days.

One of my favorite photos ever was taken shortly after we got Abby home. Paul was sitting in the recliner holding her while Cody was leaning over the arm of the chair. They are both looking at her consumed with love and amazement. She was wide-eyed, looking at them as if thinking, *Oh Lord, don't tell me I have to live with these loud guys.* Ma, Cheryl, Paul's sister, her family, and Mamaw also found her to be absolutely adorable. It had been tough waiting out those five long days, but it had been the right decision. As I had suspected would happen, the whole family fell in love with her in the first five minutes.

Over the next 18 months, Abby grew to be a beautiful little girl with lots of dark curls. She had nicknames like Thunderbutt and Curly Sue. Cody adored her. Paul and I were so happy with our sweet new child. We had to go to court on several occasions, give sworn testimony, and we had a few visits from a social worker assigned to our case. Those 18 months were challenging. It was a real blessing that the birth mother was so cooperative and true to her word; once the adoption was completed, she left us to raise our daughter.

Thinking back on the process of adoption, two Cody stories come to mind. The first occurred when the time came for the social worker to interview him. Paul and I were talking to him about the importance of telling the truth because being able to keep Abby as part of our family depended on it. He countered with, "I tell you what I am going to tell her is that those heavy things in front of that fire screen are there because that's where Daddy puts her when she is bad." He laughed loudly. The objects were there because twice wood ducks had fallen down the chimney into the den. I was in a panic.

I explained to him, "I know you think that is funny, Pal, but please, please don't tell her that. If she were to believe that crazy story, the judge would take Abby away from us." When the lady came, she was insistent on interviewing him alone. That was a very long 45 minutes for us. When she finished and we were allowed in, I had to ask, "How did it go?"

She answered, "I must tell you that he is the cutest, most well-adjusted handicapped child I have ever met. He loves his little sister. He is so personable. He even shook my hand when we finished and thanked me for interviewing him. What an impressive kid!" It was nice to breathe again.

After she was gone, Cody walked through the kitchen and grinned at me saying, "Had you worried, didn't I, Mom?"

"You are *so* not funny, Mister Smarty." Then we both laughed.

On the day of the final decree, the last and fully-binding step of the adoption, the whole family was excited. Paul, Cody, Abby, and I were to appear in the judge's chambers that morning. S.J. planned to obtain a true copy of that final decree and then cut us loose. We had a big celebration, cake, balloons, decorations, presents—the whole bit planned for that night. Close family and friends would be celebrating with us.

I had all of us well groomed as we entered the courthouse that morning. The judge had two chairs in front of his desk and a small sofa against the wall behind that. Paul sat down in one of the chairs, and Cody jumped into the other. Thinking it would not matter, Abby and I sat on the sofa. When the judge came in, he commented on what a great looking family we were. That was nice. He told us everything had gone very well, and once we were sworn in, we could complete the final adoption stage. We were all facing his desk when he said, "Raise your right hands." I could see the panic in Cody's eyes. As Paul and I followed his instructions, Cody, believing he was talking to him, raised his left hand. Cody didn't even notice the judge smile. When the session was over, the judge congratulated us and we left.

We sat on a bench in the hallway waiting for S.J. to bring our notarized copy of the decree, and Cody blurted out, "Man, it was like freaky Perry Mason in there! I almost hit the deck when he swore us in!"

I calmly told him, "First of all, he was talking to Dad and me but you jumped in my chair, so you couldn't see me behind you. The other tip for the future is, in case they are really talking to you, it might be a good idea to learn to tell your left hand from your right." We all laughed.

Abby grew to be the perfect child for our family. She adores her big brother, and they have created many funny and sometimes scary scenes. Anything from riding the four-wheeler three at a time with their cousin, John (after taking the key without permission), to Cody hiding her in the van when she was two to take her to school for show-and-tell, to telling her when undesirable grades crept into her life, "Don't worry Mom and Dad with those bad grades, just sign them yourself. You do know how to spell Raina, don't you?" He had learned that misspelling my name was a dead give away. Precious children . . . joy of our lives.

Cody started second grade that year. Mr. Charley did his part in moving the platform and greeted us at the door on day one to tell us. We appreciated that. The teacher was wonderful and helped Cody to experience a great school year. Recess was still hard to fix, but adaptive P.E. balanced that problem. The only real negative that year came with the change to a new physical therapist on his team. It started during our first IEP meeting when she said, "As soon as we stop making Cody walk and get him into a wheelchair, we will all be much happier." I had to practice great control not to lunge across the table at her. Instead, I steadied my voice and myself and delivered this message while staring dead on at her, "Let me share something with you. I have spent every waking moment for the last seven years working toward helping Cody to do as well as he does, and that includes walking. My whole family has. That includes rigid exercise programs, an array of appliances, several surgeries, and PT by one of the leading experts in this area twice a week for five years. Obviously, she thought it was well worth it. Before I agree for you to work with my child, you need to go read your job description again. That includes the part that tells you how to help children with disabilities to function in spite of their handicap." She was stunned. The whole team was. She never mentioned the wheelchair to us again. However, she did not work well with Cody. She constantly criticized us, and that made our experience with her very unpleasant. I was thankful she was only there that one year.

Third grade went smoothly. Cody progressed very well. The only outstanding event that year was one morning when I got a call from Cody saying he needed me to bring some forgotten papers to school. He needed the papers to prevent him from getting a zero on an assignment. When I arrived, he was sitting in the office looking like he had lost his best friend. I knelt down and implored, "What's wrong, Pal? Did you get fussed at?"

He said, "No ma'am, but my day is absolutely ruined."

Thinking I had brought bail, my message was, "Here are your papers. You are rescued!"

"Not hardly. That is not the problem."

"Well, what is it? You can tell Mom."

He looked at me so seriously and said, "The substitute's ugly." Sarcastically, I proclaimed, "Well, by cracky, I may have to take you out of this school if they can't start bringing in cute substitutes!" He grinned, gave me a big hug, and returned to class. What a character!

Fourth grade was also fairly uneventful. Although medical problems occurred from time to time, Cody continued under the care of five doctors, and he was thriving. He signed our names to a few papers with low grades and brought home an 8x10 picture of Misty when school pictures came in. I solved those two problems: I told him that forgery was a federal offense with mandatory jail time (leaving out the fact that there are no 9-year-olds on crutches in jail), and I had him return the picture to Misty. I explained that I was sure her family had ordered that for themselves, and they could hide the love message she had written to him on the back of the picture.

I do remember that Christmas when Cody was in the fourth grade. I asked, "What do you want for Christmas, Son?"

He said, "Either a bird or to walk without crutches and braces."

I cried later to think how he thought Santa could bring brace- or crutch-free walking, then laughed to think a bird could outweigh the importance of losing his disability.

He joined Boy Scouts that year. I never realized we were signing up for a part-time job. They did a world of good, but there was a lot of work involved—putting bags out for the canned food drive on a Saturday and going back the next Saturday and picking them up. On one occasion, Paul was helping him with that and somehow let the wheelchair go without locking the wheels. When he turned around, Cody was hollering because the wheelchair had rolled and slid down that steep, icy driveway into the ditch. Paul just scooped him up after they had a belly laugh, and they continued with their mission. There were also blue and gold banquets and many chores for earning badges.

My favorite was the Mom-and-Me Camp Out. For us, it was one boy and one servant. It always rains ten inches while you are pitching the tent, and I pushed the wheelchair through deep red mud for three days, while the Eagle Scouts politely spoke when they passed us on the muddy trail. We still managed to have a lot of fun, even when I got in a boat with two of the boys in his troop, and Cody rowed us out to the middle of the lake. Then I laughed while they rowed us around in circles for thirty minutes until they finally got the idea of teamwork. When they gave me the iron-on transfer that read, "I survived Mom-and-Me" to put on my tee shirt, I told them it was about ten feet too small. Cody made new friends and had wonderful values re-enforced through Scouts. The core values of Scouts include things like courage and perseverance. It wasn't easy to participate in activities like camping out and climbing trails, etc., but it was important because their motto is, "Do your best."

On a Saturday morning in the year when Cody was 9 years old and Abby was two, Ma decided she wanted to take her only two grandchildren on an outing without help. I was hesitant about that idea because a child with leg braces and arm crutches as his only method of walking and one in the "terrible twos" can create quite a challenge for a grandmother alone on her adventure. Ma was insistent, so I agreed. That stressful morning would become one of the most memorable and amusing memories ever for Ma, for all of us.

The agenda Ma had worked out was to go to McDonalds and all three of them eat breakfast together then journey on to the mall to go shopping. The plan seemed doable, but we didn't realize what a rip "Curley Sue" was on that morning. Ma and Cody were soon to witness the manifestation of toddler energy and curiosity.

When the time came to load into the car, I went out in the driveway and helped Ma get Cody strapped in one of the middle seats of her mini van and Abby buckled into the car seat that was secured in the other one. All three of them were happy and excited about their planned trip. That would soon change.

As they drove away that morning, after soliciting promises from both of my children to behave and stay close to Ma, I shuddered. The whole idea made me nervous, but I longed for the bond between my mother and my children to be strong. Plus, it was the first time since Abby's birth I could remember anyone offering me three hours of peace and quiet. As much as I treasure the gift of time spent with my children, a break would have also been a gift. It just never happened. Only forty-five minutes after their departure, in the middle of a major "cleaning house without kids" project, they returned and Ma deposited them on the porch and left. Apparently, she was speechless. I was left to hear the story from Cody.

Cody explained that on the way to McDonalds on a very busy road that connects to the interstate, for reasons unknown to him, Abby decided to unbuckle the car seat and slide the side door to the mini van open while traveling at high speed. Ma slammed on the brakes, got out in the middle of heavy traffic, walked around the front of the car, buckled Abby back into the car seat, and slammed the door. She then walked back into heavy traffic, got back in her seat, and journeyed on to McDonalds. (I wasn't sure at that moment who was more dangerous, Ma or Abby.) After giving the kids a lecture and obtaining from them a promise of good behavior, she committed to carrying through with their plans. I'm just not sure she understood that toddler promises are never very reliable. She would soon find that out in a most dynamic way.

Ma bought breakfast for all three in her little party, sat down, and began to have a nice meal and conversation with Cody. While they were visiting, Abby decided, again for reasons unknown, to pour a large cup of coffee into Ma's purse. Most of that hot brown liquid landed on her checkbook. That must have been Ma's limit because she drained her purse as well as she could, loaded them up, drove the half-mile back to our house, and left them on our front porch. She did not say a word to me. Cody came in laughing hysterically as he told this tale, but revealed when he could that the funniest part was that it was the first time he had ever heard Ma say a curse word. I was so proud to know that the only thing that could drive my dear mother to use profanity was an outing with my sweet little girl. Oh well, bad nerves, ruined checks, but precious memories.

On one occasion, Misty was spending the weekend with her elderly grandmother. She and Cody had been on the phone talking a lot that day. That evening, as we were preparing to go to the college football game, Cody came carrying the portable phone into the room where I was, saying, "Misty's grandma wants to talk to you."

I had never spoken to her before, but this was the shaky message, "Honey, I am sorry if I upset Cody about the ballgame, but when Misty is with us, we just don't let her go off with boys at night."

My reply was, "Ma'am, I don't know what Cody has told you, but I assure you we don't allow our nine-year-old son to date. I am so sorry he upset you." Cody's explanation was, "Well, Mom, it was worth a try."

Another thing he thought was worth a try happened one night, at the age of ten, when he and Bart were spending the night with Ma. They saw on TV where you could find out your future by calling the Psychic Hotline. Those little ten-year-old boys were very interested in their futures, so they plotted to stay up until 4 A.M. and call. Cody felt he should call first since it was his grandmother's phone. First, it cost $10 for them to tell him another number to call. The person at the second number asked his age for an additional $10. He was too scared to lie, so he told her his real birth date. That brought on the "You have to be 18 or older to call" speech. Bart went through the same process. All total, the fee was $40, and they had not even heard their fortunes. When the phone bill came in, I confronted them and got a full confession. Of course, it would have been very hard for them to deny because we all knew my dear 64-year-old mother would not be up at 4 A.M. calling the

Psychic Hotline. Bart begged me not to tell his mom, so I made them work it off. From then on, I kept a closer eye on those two.

The principal summed that year up well at Award's Day, as Cody's group was returning to their chairs, chewing gum, sloppy, shoes untied, clowning as usual. "The very best thing you can say about fourth graders is that next year they will be fifth graders."

We did have a few downs then, as the smart-mouth syndrome began to develop. On a day when that got to be a problem and I was short on discipline ideas, I stopped the car at a stop sign. In the middle of his mouthing off, I demanded, "Get out!"

He looked shocked and said, "Huh?"

I repeated, "Get out and walk home." There was dead silence followed by laughter. I said, "Scared you, huh?"

He exclaimed, "You sure did! I'm sorry I smarted off." Well, it worked that once anyway.

In the summer before Cody entered the sixth grade he was healthy and walking well in leg braces with arm crutches. He had a portable wheelchair, but it was only used for long distances and whenever he was exhausted. I made an appointment with Dr. D. to discuss surgery on his right leg. That leg rotated out, and we felt if it were turned in by surgery that it would enable him to walk so much better. When we went to the doctor that day and asked our options concerning that leg, he said, "Cody has done extremely well with all of his surgeries and de-rotating that leg would probably help him to walk better. However, when you operate in an area where there is paralysis, there is a completely new set of risks. Neither the skin nor the blood supply is good. The bones will heal much slower. That leg was turned out in utero. I am not sure we can fix it. If you insist, we can try it. I just want to make sure you are aware of the potential problems."

"Pride goes before destruction."[14] I had my mind set on fixing that leg. My thought was, *Oh they have to tell you there is a risk of death before they sew up a half-inch cut on your finger. He said it himself, he has done well with all of the previous surgeries, and he will do well this time too.* Cody, Paul, and the rest of the family trusted my judgment. That was a mistake in this matter. I wanted that leg fixed, and where disabilities are concerned, you just can't fix everything. I knew Dr. D would not have told me there were extra risks if he was not concerned.

...ened. I should have put Cody's happiness and well-
...desire for him to walk better. It was too risky. I signed
...The surgery was set for July 3.

...ght we had adjusted our sails, but we were wrong. The
...hat surgery, in spite of the doctor's warnings, drove us
...orm as ugly as sin. In fact, you could describe the results
... once heard a preacher describe sin:

> *It takes you farther than you ever want to go,*
> *It keeps you longer than you ever want to stay,*
> *It costs you more than you ever want to pay.*

...cost of that decision for Cody was three long years of tor-
...end, his right leg had permanent damage, his ability to walk
much again was gone, and all of us had been forced to learn how to heal
from the inside out.

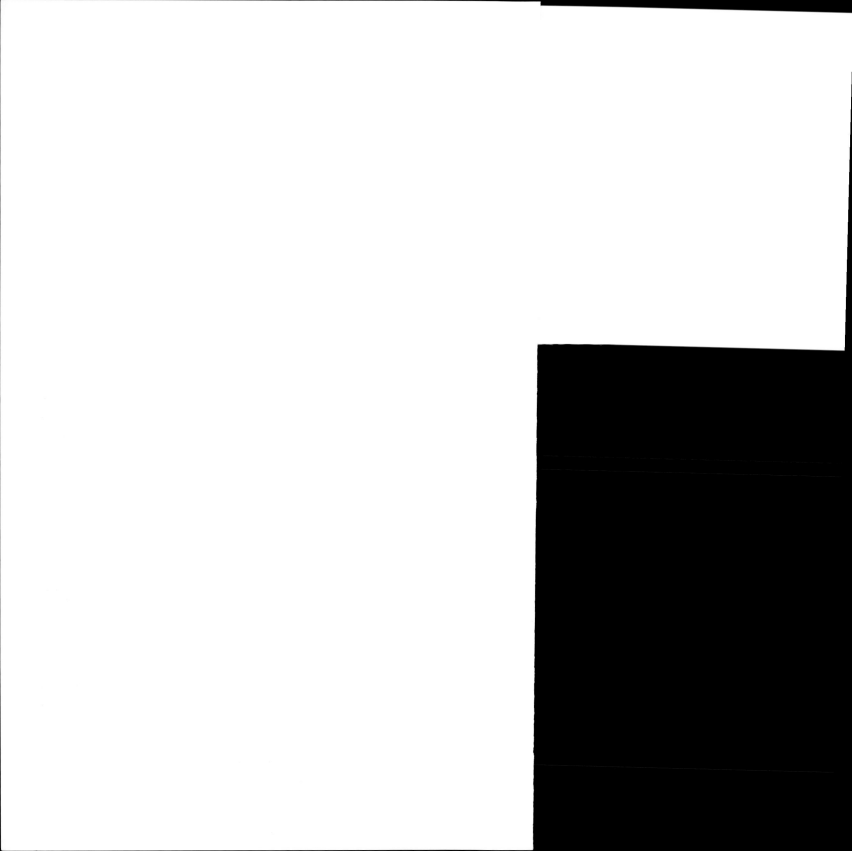

Raina Futrell

Email: codyandraina@yahoo

Jimmy Davis continued to sing that song as long as he lived, and he lived to be over 100 years old. One of my favorite NICU stories of all time is about a tiny, premature baby girl who was dying. Her five-year-old brother was allowed to come into the unit because the baby's team felt she would not survive the night, and he had been so insistent that he had something he needed to share with her. He went to her bedside, took her tiny hand in his small hand, and sang "You Are My Sunshine" to her. She made a miraculous recovery, and all of the witnesses, including the doctors, said the only possible explanation was her brother's heartfelt message in song. Cody would soon need all of our songs and prayers.

I wish now that when we went to check into the hospital on that hot July 3 that we had all had the feeling Paul had experienced the morning of the shunt surgery—that terrible feeling in the pit of your stomach that tells you not to go through with something. Instead, we were excited about the idea that Cody's leg would finally be straight. The only thing that was straight about it was that it sent us straight into a disaster.

"The surgery went well," was the remark by the doctor. We were so happy and basked in our false sense of security. Of course, when Cody returned to the room, there was that familiar shock factor of his paleness and weakness. In this case, there was the huge cast with three large pins poking out of each side of his right leg. After a few hours though he began to rally, and we felt the surgery had been a big success.

go home so Cody wouldn't have to spend a holiday in the hospital. The clouding of my judgment by being his mother was synonymous with the clouded judgment of insurance companies that are in the business of collecting as much revenue as possible. It's akin to what I say about some school systems now. They are teaching standardized tests and forgetting about the children. In this case, with us and everyone involved, other issues overshadowed optimal care for the patient, and his outcome was evidence of that.

At home, Cody seemed to be wiped out most of the time. After a few weeks, we went to the doctor's office, and he took the pins out. I thought those pins had been painful, and Cody would be better after they were out, but it didn't happen. Near the end of the six weeks when he was supposed to be able to return to school, it became obvious that was not going to be possible.

On the advice and recommendations of friends, the school system helped me to obtain Ms. Ann, a homebound teacher who would become another "angel among us." Isn't it amazing how your conception of what a service consists of and the truth about that service can be so different? For some reason, we had the impression that the homebound teacher would come every day and teach what he had missed at school that day. Not even close. She was wonderful, but she was loaded down with homebound students. Granted, most of her load consisted of pregnant students or those who had been expelled from school but were not old enough yet to drop out of school permanently.

Cody quickly became one of her favorite students. He loved her too, but the shock was that she was only allowed to come for one and a half hours twice a week. On those visits, she brought a huge stack of work and assignments, monitored his taking exams, and hauled out folders of work he had completed between visits. If my sister had not been a schoolteacher the first three years after she graduated from college, had not had a job with flexible hours, and had not been a doting aunt willing to spend hours on end helping him, we would never have been able to keep up.

Schoolwork or the surgery or the cast, I wasn't sure what it was, but something was keeping him down. Cody was pale, continuously tired, irritable, and even he could not explain it. We had lived through many surgeries and casts. Before, he had always bounced back within days of being discharged from the hospital. We didn't know what it was, but we knew something was not right. The only real clue was the swelling in his leg. After every other bone surgery and applied cast, the cast would be almost flopping off within 48 hours. This one remained tight. We kept his leg elevated on a pillow on the extended, raised-leg plate of his rented wheelchair or on his bed 24 hours a day. I was so upset and worried and went to the doctor the day his cast was to be removed with resolve to have his team locate the culprit. We didn't have to look far. As soon as that cast was removed, we saw it. On top of his ankle, there was a rectangular area about 2"x4." It was as black as midnight. A wave of horror rolled across me. Around that black scab was all that swelling. My fear switched to an action gear. "What do we do?"

The doctor said, "Help him into the tub and soak it twice a day in real warm water. When the scab comes off, we will clean it up and see what we do from there." Cody and I were silent on the way home. I knew he was as scared as I was, but it was one of the few times in our lives we just were not ready to talk about it. I prayed and for a few minutes, I really wanted to place blame. *Why hadn't they cut a window in the cast? Why hadn't we demanded the cast be removed sooner so we could see what was under it?* I even thought for a brief moment, *Why hadn't Cody demanded attention to that leg?* Right behind those thoughts came reality. *He doesn't have enough feeling in that area to pinpoint the problem. I am the one that should have demanded more attention to that leg.*

Then the big brick hit me, the one that would haunt me for years, for forever really, *I should have listened to Dr. D when he warned me of the possible problems from operating on an area where paralysis was present. Why hadn't I listened?* One thing was for sure; I would suffer for my haughtiness for a long time. Sadly, so would Cody.

When we arrived home, the family got upset upon hearing our report, but Ma, Paul, and Cheryl, all made commitments to help get Cody's leg well. None of us had a clue what it would really take. As I think back now I am reminded of something a surviving officer of the Titanic said the morning after that disaster, "It's a good thing God doesn't let us see the end, or we would never make the journey we are supposed to make in this life." [16]

We were about to embark on a journey that would almost do us all in.

We helped Cody in and out of that tub and re-splinted that leg twice a day for only a few days. He was so sick. One night he got into the tub, and about five minutes later, he screamed for me to come there. I ran wildly to the tub area and found that his right leg was floating at the top of the water. So ugly, so swollen, so scary. I got him out, and he looked at me through those dark circles around his eyes and pleaded, "Mom, please help me. I have tried to get better, but I am really sick."

The tears gushed from my eyes as I told him, "Son . . . Son, this is not your fault. It's mine, the insurance rules that sent you home too early, the team's, anybody's but yours. We can't even afford to waste time trying to see whose fault it is. I promise you this; we will go there tomorrow and demand help. Whatever it takes, however long it takes, we will get you well."

Then he asked one of the hardest questions ever, "Mom, do you think I am going to lose my leg?"

I was almost paralyzed myself by that question, but I was not about to let his little, depressed self in on that secret, so I mustered all the courage I had left and told him, "Not a chance, Buddy. I will take you to Houston, New York, or Kingdom Come before I let that happen. You go to bed and get some sleep and rest assured that your mom will go on a mission starting first thing in the morning that will end with your leg like new and you up walking better than ever."

I was sincere, and he was relieved. I just didn't know that even with all the help I could assemble, his leg would never be the same. We would eventually have to exchange that rented wheelchair for one of his own. That night I was awake almost the entire night crying and praying. I looked in on Cody several times to discover he was asleep, a restless, fitful sleep, but sleep. That night I began a useless process that would take me years to escape, emotionally beating myself up, blaming myself for all of Cody's problems. Looking back now, I can advise people not to do that. It kept me wiped out and did not help one scintilla in the healing process of Cody's leg. You can't go back. What's done is done, and it just can't be undone. If you sit and wallow in the "I wish I could go back" or the "if only we had" or the "why didn't we notice" phraseology, you will only become a useless shell of a person. The only helpful thing you can do is set out the options before you, pick the best one (after obtaining the advice of experts on whatever issue you are addressing), reach way down inside yourself, gather whatever courage you have left while looking around and gathering your best supporters, and rip right into the storm head on.

The next day I took Cody to the doctor with new resolve. Something must be done about his leg. Dr. D. wanted to continue the tub soaks. I was not going to agree to that. In all of our seventeen years of dealing with Cody's orthopedic issues, it was the only time we were ever at odds. I crossed my arms and unloaded, "You will have to lock us up in this building tonight. I am not leaving until we put into action a plan to fix his leg."

He replied in a sort of angry tone, "Okay, I am going to send you to see J.W."

I snapped back with, "Who is she and what are her credentials?" I was not going to let anyone who was not fully qualified in wound care touch that leg. Turns out she was not only fully qualified, she was God-sent. He explained that she was a wound care nurse in an outpatient facility connected to them and had a great success rate with healing wounds. Cody and I felt better. We had been given a consult with an expert. We had no idea that she would become another angel in our lives and a very dear friend.

The next afternoon we went to the building where J.W. worked, a facility we had never been to before. A hint of her dedication to her patients surfaced when, surprisingly, she met us in the lobby. She and Cody formed an immediate attachment. I was not myself because of the fear and anxiety I was experiencing over that leg. Really, I guess I unloaded on her all of our frustrations over his lack of progress. I was sorry for that when I found out how kind and sensitive she was, but it was September and the surgery had been on July 3. It was time for action. Cody and I saw action in a most dynamic form as soon as Ms. J. looked at that wound. She was alarmed, but in an effort to keep Cody from a state of panic she said only, "We have some work to do. First, before anything else, I am going to call Dr. D. and tell him the scab has to come off, and then we will work from there." I liked her confidence. I liked the way she protected Cody's feelings. I suspected she was a very dedicated, conscientious nurse. I was right. As it turned out, her loyalty and dedication would be the savior of both Cody's leg and of our sanity.

We returned to Dr. D. and he incised and removed that scab in a surgical manner. That opened up the Pandora's box of infection and drainage. Over the following four-month period, Ms. J very carefully, meticulously worked at getting that wound to heal. She was fabulous, an artist at work. It was interesting that the main substance she used looked like the fiberglass insulation you usually see between the boards framing a house prior to floating sheet rock walls, but it was actually made from seaweed. In reading research for nursing projects and research on spina bifida, I am always amazed how many times cures are found from substances in nature.

The four months were touch-and-go. On one of our appointment days with Dr. D., he was gone and a doctor we had never met was there. He said, "I am going to stop all the wound care you are doing and send you to New Orleans to use the hyperbaric chamber. You will probably have to sell your house to pay for it, but his leg will get well."

I took Cody home to rest. That doctor had done a thorough exam, and at that point, the wound was very deep and painful. I set out in a storm to try to fill the prescriptions that he had said were so critical to begin using that night. After going to five pharmacies without success, I had a melt down. I went home and Ms. J had left three messages, anxious to hear what had happened during our visit. I wanted to tell her, too, and hear her reaction. Her reaction was, "Why don't you wait until Dr. D. gets back on Monday and see what he says? That prescription is a formula for vinegar. That is the treatment a lot of doctors used to use for those type wounds." Vinegar? Was he crazy?

I told her, "Thanks, friend, for knowing your job so well and for caring so much. Thank you for bringing your old friend back to reality."

That day was not the saddest I ever was over that wound, but it was the most mad I ever felt over it. The nerve of that guy! Dr. D. apologized and gave us the okay to continue what we had been doing. Everyone involved was thankful. Ms. J. is the type of nurse who steals a huge place in your heart forever. She sure did in Cody's and mine. So did Dr. D. and his entire staff.

Four months after our first visit to Ms. J., she called and said to me, "Guess what?"

"We don't have to come anymore?"

Her response was, "You don't have to come anymore. He will always have a scar, but over time, with good skin care, it will get better. He is a precious child. I am so glad I had a chance to meet and work with y'all." We let her know that it was she who was loved and appreciated, and without her, Cody's leg would have been doomed. You never forget angels in your life like Ms. J. We took her a thank-you and had a tearful departure. Little did we know that would be only the tip of the iceberg, and we would come to understand why there is a saying in Malaysia:

Just because the river is quiet, does not mean the alligators have left.[17]

We enjoyed the holiday season and were so thankful the wound was healed. Still, Cody was not his usual happy self. I thought of all the reasons that could be. I thought, *He is probably just wiped out from the last six months. He may be dreading physical therapy and learning to walk again. He is probably concerned about catching up in school. He is about to be a teenager.* We wanted it to be anything but more problems with that leg.

When the holidays were over, we set a schedule for physical therapy twice a week to help Cody to regain strength in his legs and to regain his walking ability. He returned to school. It sounds redundant, but it's true; he never rallied. His teacher for sixth grade was my friend who had been his teacher in the first and fourth grades also. I was so thankful that she was familiar with his equipment, and I could count on her letting me know if any problems arose. We had no idea how soon and with what terrible consequences those problems would appear.

Only four weeks into school, I received one of those Cody's-in-trouble- calls at work one afternoon. The school secretary called my office, and when I answered she said, "Ms. K. needs to talk to you about Cody." My heart began to flutter. That was one time I hoped it was about a discipline problem, but I knew better.

She came on the line and these are the words I heard, "Raina, Cody collapsed in the room a few minutes ago, and he can't walk at all. He seems okay and is sitting on the desk talking to the other kids, but when you touch his right knee, it burns your hand through his jeans."

My lone comment was, "I'm on my way."

I am not sure how I managed to see through the tears to drive to that school, or how I kept from having an accident, but God got me there safely. Cody was sitting on a desk entertaining the other kids but touching his right knee burned my hand through his jeans and his ankle was dangling oddly. The right leg from the knee down was swollen to double its normal size. I dried the tears and panic took their place, but for Cody's sake, I tried not to show it. I put him in the portable wheelchair I kept in my van and drove straight to the emergency room. I had them call Dr. D. We were routed from there to his office. They had done blood work at the hospital; they did x-rays at his office. There was bad news from both. His ankle was broken and his white blood cell count was very high, indicative of infection. They casted his leg and scheduled us for IV antibiotics to start the next morning. I suggested, "Since his leg feels like fire, I think we should start them now." On second thought, they agreed.

We headed from there to meet with the "on call" nurse at the same facility where we had received wound care. She was to start the IV and antibiotics. Entering the building, we had to pass the after-hours clinic. I believe God sends people to you when you need them. He sure did on that occasion. In that clinic was Ms. J., whom we had not seen since she discharged us one month before that. She had brought her son there because he had a sore throat. She saw us pass by and came out immediately to see what was going on. When we told her, she had the same reaction as the first time she met us. It was the same as St. Nick in the old Christmas story . . . she "spoke not a word but went straight to 'her' work."[18] She called her husband to come and get their son and then called the "on call" nurse and told her she would take care of her little buddy. Thank God for rescuers like her.

Earlier Cody had won a state contest by writing and submitting a tape of a song played on his violin. He had then been asked to come to the state capital, four hours away, and play that song at the state-wide PTA teachers' banquet. We went to the clinic that morning and got Cody's meds and told Ms. J. about it. We rolled on to the pharmacy after that and got enough bags of IV meds to get through the weekend. Cody had a heparin lock IV and a big, casted right leg. When we got to the van, there was a package leaning against the back door of the van, a package that looked like a sectional fishing pole. Instead, it was a portable IV pole. We knew Ms. J. had left it. God bless her. We both wished all nurses could be like her.

We went to that PTA convention, and in between meetings we would go back to the hotel room, and I would hook up his med. Paul would stand and hold that IV med bag on the pole for two hours. Cody played his song beautifully for those teachers and got a standing ovation when he was done. We couldn't hide the big cast, but the IV lock was under his sleeve and only the family and Ms. J. ever knew it was there.

We finished that round of IV meds, and his leg healed. He returned to school to finish the last few weeks. He passed, and we said goodbye to grammar school after eight years (including preschool). There had been quite a few challenges, but he had made it. However, the challenges of the leg and school were just beginning.

Now no one told me that at age twelve someone takes your child and leaves an alien for you to finish raising. We found that out as he entered junior high school. To start with, the building was two stories and there was no elevator. All of the seventh grade classes were scheduled upstairs, including Cody's. At first four coaches carried him up and down the stairs four times a day. We kept asking for a better plan, refusing once again to consider the inappropriate resource classes. By the time two months went by, the coaches were complaining of backaches.

That magically got the administration to move his classes downstairs when my cries about danger and Cody's daily humiliation had not. After that, everyone was happier. Well, there may have been one or two upset teachers, but it was done. I wondered what their attitude would have been if it had been one of their own teenagers going through that experience.

The episode that sticks out most in my mind about junior high happened when I went to pick Cody up one afternoon after school and could not find him. He was nowhere near where he was supposed to be, and after searching for twenty minutes, I spotted him sitting on a bench down by the practice field watching football practice. I had never seen him look quite as sad as he did that day. It hit me the same as a surprise ton of bricks would have. I knew he would have given anything to be out there practicing with those guys. That hurt. That really, really hurt. I waited until I regained composure before I drove down there and picked him up. He pretended to be fine. I knew better. Nothing much was said, but I silently vowed that when his leg was better we would find sports that he could handle besides baseball. I kept that vow.

During those years, the members of his Challenger Baseball team introduced him to something called G.U.M.B.O., which stands for "Games Uniting Mind and Body." GUMBO is field and track events for physically challenged kids. He has competed in that for several years now and excels in power sports—the shot put and the discus. He has broken several records that helped him to compete in the National Wheelchair Sports competitions.

We met a lady through G.U.M.B.O., Ms. P., who has been a real blessing to him where wheelchair sports are concerned. At one point, she asked me to bring him to an Air Force base 100 miles away on a Saturday so he could watch a wheelchair basketball game. Before that game was done, Cody whispered to me, "Let's go. I can't stand this."

I was shocked, thinking that he hated the sport, but once in the car he explained, "I can't stand to sit and watch that. I have got to find a way to play." So he did. He tried out for and made a high school team where he met new friends and a wonderful man, Coach G. Cody was also scouted for a college team, but has decided to go to the university in our town where they are going to give him a chance to establish wheelchair basketball. If he is able to get that accomplished, it will be the first college team in our state.

Altogether, Cody had eight stress fractures in those three years. Those included two fractures in his left leg, indicating that leg would not support him either. Once he even had a red cast from his hip to his toes on the right side. Abby would not go near him. She kept saying it looked like blood. One day my sister called me from her cell phone and told me she and Cody had been in a wreck and his IV had bent backwards. It turned out he was okay, but when the police saw the IV and the cast, they were not sure what to think of that. No danger of breaking his right leg, it was already a done deal. After that scare, I took family medical leave until he was better.

That Christmas we presented Cody with a gift I said we would never buy. Because of his current situation, we had to. It was a sports wheelchair. He was so delighted, and I was so sad. He felt like he had been set free. I felt like I had spent thirteen years of our lives teaching him to walk, and it was the biggest personal failure of my life. I was wrong. Sometimes life just takes you where you don't expect to ever go, and accepting that is a struggle.

During the entire calamity over his leg, we had even gone to a different doctor. We were all so frustrated. It was an arrangement where they took insurance and charged nothing beyond that. Considering the amount the two and a half years had cost, it was almost mandated. The best synopsis of it would be, it was the most inadequate care we ever received and the most expensive "free care" I ever heard of. By that, I mean it was two hours away. Some 7 A.M. appointments forced us to go the night before. Over the short trial period, between hotels, flat tires, dead batteries, gas, and meals, we spent more than we ever spent in a year supplementing our insurance. Even worse, we just did not jive with the staff there. Upon leaving, Cody was screaming at me that he should never be made to walk again. A lot of that was the poorly fitted braces, which had pinched blood blisters on his leg. The extreme rudeness of the brace guy was coupled with the teenage hormone syndrome, but I didn't realize it. I declared, "Okay, Cody. I give up. I am going to stop and throw all of your equipment in the trash. I give in. End of discussion."

He went into a panic. "Mom, I've never heard you say that

before, never. Please, don't give up. I'll be nothing if you stop pushing me. Please don't ever say that again!" It scared him into continuing to try to do his best. That's all I was asking.

Our best is really all that any of us can do, whether it's a handi-capped kid or the parents trying to raise that child. Giving in to the wheelchair seemed like admitting failure to me—but to Cody it opened up a whole new world. It was the first time in his life that he could move faster than the people around him. People would see us in the mall and tell me, "You are the one who is handicapped." The chair also sent him into a world of sports in which he could compete on a level play-ing field. All of those years of walking helped him to build tremendous strength and endurance and kept him from having some of the health problems that can stem from sitting all of the time. I thought we were working toward crutch-free walking some day. All of the stress fractures let me know that wasn't going to happen, and for a long time I couldn't get past that. What I finally realized was that as parents, we have certain jobs to do, but we are really just guardians on their journey. If you try to live only your hopes and dreams, the child will be lost. The harsh reality was that Cody didn't want to walk anymore. He wanted to roll. He was tired, and he loved that quick-moving wheelchair. I realized that the only thing being accomplished by forcing him to continue trying to walk was ruining his bones and our relationship. He still couldn't walk. Encouraging a child to do his best is one thing, trying to force him to accomplish goals that *you* dream can be quite another.

Finally, I put my trust where it should have been all along, in God and Cody. Once the forced walking sessions stopped, as has been the pattern of his entire life, Cody went on to accomplish wonderful feats from the wheelchair. It's his life, and I had to start letting him live it.

The last big episode with his leg required eight weeks of anti-biotics. Cody was more depressed than I had ever seen him. It was just unfortunate for all of us that a three-year medical crisis and teenage craziness collided. On top of that, one day about two weeks from com-pleting his last round of antibiotics, Cody told me on the way home, "Mom, I am itching a little." He was sitting in the second set of seats in the van because of his big cast, so I turned around and his arm was a solid whelp.

I called Ms. J. on the cell phone and asked, "Did we use anything different today? Prep solution, tourniquet, tape, anything have latex in it?"

Her reply was, "No."

"Then, Houston, we have a problem. He has developed an allergic reaction to this drug too."

She said, "I'll call Dr. D. and let you know what he says." He and his nurse worked so hard and were so good to their patients. I knew one of them would respond right away. He did. Ms. J. called back shortly after we arrived home with the instructions on how much of what drug to give.

Well, we were due to leave at 7 A.M. the next morning to go to a Challenger Baseball game 100 miles away. Ms. J. wanted me to call her at her house before we left at 6:45 A.M. on a Saturday and tell her how he was. This is the message I left, "No rash. Just this side of an anti-allergy medication coma, headed to try and focus enough to hit a baseball." He was so sleepy, but he hit two grand slams.

That night I gave him the IV med thirty minutes after I had given him the anti-allergy medicine, and an hour later he was in his room and yelled that call that always makes me jump out of my skin, "Mom, you better come look." This time the whelps were from the neck to the toes.

I called Ms. J. and she called the pharmacist to see what we could do. The pharmacist told her, "Are y'all crazy? That boy will be wheezing next. You have to call the doctor!" She snapped us both back into reality that night. It wouldn't matter how many drugs he had developed reactions to, he could not take any more of that one. So we agreed to meet at the clinic early on Sunday morning and call Dr. D. I watched Cody very carefully through the night. The whelps went away, but the frustration was building.

The next morning we met and Ms. J. paged Dr. D. He answered right away. She was only on the line a few minutes, then turned to me and reported, "Well, y'all are on the big guns now." That was an expression for using antibiotics with more potential for harmful side effects, but with the capacity to destroy hard-to-kill infections. I knew this one could harm his hearing and/or his kidneys. It was one of those times when you have to pick a less than desirable treatment to get to the desirable outcome. We were at the end of a three-year episode of infections and bone breaks. It had to stop.

Ten minutes after the medicine started to infuse, Cody started clawing his head and said he felt like fire ants were crawling all over him. Almost at the same time, his neck started turning red in a rising pattern like a thermometer. I looked at Ms. J. in astonishment, and she explained that it was called the redneck syndrome. She asked, "What do you want to do?"

I exclaimed, "I want to be on another planet! You do what you normally do to stop it." She slowed the rate way down, and within minutes, the itching ceased and the red crept right back down his neck. We all felt like we had been on a ride on the Apollo 13 space ship. I told Ms. J. how thankful we were for her knowledge and skills and then added, "I tell you, Ms. J., I have never seen anything like that in my life. I thought the redneck syndrome was when you lived on the other side of the river." (It was a joke often made by other area high schools.) She laughed.

That drug hardened his veins, and by then I was starting all of his IV's. That was almost every dose. In addition, we had to worry about his hearing. Being the comedian he was, he started responding at first to everything we asked him with, "Huh? What did y'all say?"

We answered him each time in unison with, "You are so not funny."

However, the sticks, the pain, and the confinement, all began to wear us down. When the levels that were run dictated that we had to start giving it twice a day, Cody and I both fell apart. Ms. J. rescued us both. She is the sweetest, most wonderful person and nurse you could ever ask for. Cody was so depressed and irritable he was scaring us. So we decided that counseling, while a very good and necessary idea, would have to be introduced to him slowly.

After we started the slow infusion of the medicine one afternoon, T. came in. Ms. J. said, "Cody, I want you to meet one of my closest friends." T. began to talk to him while we slowly backed out of the room, one through each door, and gently closed the doors behind us.

We had never left him before. As I exited, I caught a glimpse of Cody's face—his eyes had grown huge, and he looked shocked.

When an anxious hour had passed, I went back to get him. T. was young, cute, and personable, and I was expecting him to be friends with her by then. Instead, he looked very angry. As we were taking the IV line out, I asked him, "What's wrong, Son?"

"Nothing. Let's go." Then he whispered in my ear, "I'll tell you in the car." He wasn't about to act ugly in front of Ms. J.; at least there was that.

As soon as he was in, the wheelchair was loaded, and I had started the car, he unloaded, "You and Ms. J. think y'all are so smart leaving me in there a whole hour with a dang psychiatrist. I am not going to have it!"

I said as kindly as I could, "She is not a psychiatrist, Honey. She is a counselor, and we thought it might help you to feel better if you talked to her." He exclaimed loudly, "Don't try to fool me! When they start asking 'How do you feel about this and how do you feel about that?' they are a dad gum psychiatrist!" When I got home and he went to his room, I called Ms. J. and told her what verbal abuse I had endured. We laughed. It felt good to laugh.

T. continued to meet with Cody over the next few weeks during his IV and therapy sessions. I loved T's methods, no drugs, no hypnosis, just kind listening and scriptures and control exercises. While T. worked with Cody, Ms. J. was my counselor.

As quickly as the depression started, it ended. The angels in our lives helped us; Cody's relief when we allowed him to have the wheelchair helped, and I felt an urgent desire to stop circling the drain and move forward into new adventures.

In the end, the leg was finally healed, we had all formed lifelong friendships, and Cody had developed such an attachment to T. that even after the sessions were ended, he would sometimes say kidding, "Mom, I'm depressed. I need to go see T."

"Son, give me a break!" Then we would laugh.

The truth is that God planted angels in our paths like Ms. J. and T. to help the wound and us to heal from the inside out. They have a big ol' place in our hearts and always will.

When I picked Cody up from junior high on the last day, I looked behind us to make sure no one was running out to say, "Wait! Come back! You don't really get to move on to high school." He had made several new friends, met a neat counselor, and been introduced to choir. Singing in school and church choirs would become a continuous blessing in his life. The young lady who was the junior high choir director had been a good influence in his life. We just thanked God we were out of there and moving on. The leg problems and the stairs had made junior high barely doable.

That summer he went to med camp for a week. While packing, he told us, "We will probably stay up all night, every night. You know how us handicaps are."

I told Paul, "I do believe he thinks it is a club he has joined instead of a birth defect."

It was a strange feeling that fall on the first day of orientation at the high school. As we sat in freshmen orientation in the auditorium, some things had changed. Styles, of course, were very different. When Paul and I were students there in the '70s, nobody wore jeans and flip-flops to school. Of course, now our biggest concern for Cody was making his way around among the other 2200 students there. We should have known he would be okay. He had a wonderful group of counselors and principals. The counselor he loved most, Ms. L., kept a close eye on him in high school. She was always sensitive to issues that could have caused him a lot of embarrassment. Because of her great personality and talents, she was chosen to move on to the university to be in charge of recruiting before Cody graduated from high school. How glad we are of that. It was all the recruiting the university would need to do to hook Cody.

He immediately made an impression on the high school adaptive PE coach and on all the coaches. I saw one of the assistant principals in the hall about two weeks after school started, and he said to me, "I told Cody I was going to meet him in the parking lot this afternoon to race him in that sports wheelchair. Of course I'll be in my truck." The leaders and kids in that school embraced him and helped him to survive mass confusion.

Last year on Awards Day, he was given the Good Citizenship Award by the American Legion. Ma had received that same award 50 years before when she was a senior in high school. She presented hers to

Cody in what was a very moving moment for the whole family. She felt she had gone full circle with her life, and the bond grew even stronger between her and her only grandson. It was one of those rare, magical moments in life—a moment you never forget and are so thankful you were privileged to witness.

The reality is that Cody is a world-class athlete. He is headed to college to get a degree in radio and TV broadcasting, and hopefully, he is on his way to being a famous sports announcer. He drives a truck with hand controls and plans to get married and have a family when he has finished his college education.

Little by little, we clawed our way out of that pit we fell into when Cody was born, the pit of spina bifida, the pit of no normal baby, and no perfect child. There are many pits in life, especially ones that teenagers fall into. Drinking, drugs, elicit sex, eating disorders, computer addictions, and on and on and on. Sometimes we create those pits for them because we teach them their bodies have to be perfect as though popularity is the only thing that counts. We teach them how to play ball, cheer, dance, and sing, but often we are not too worried about teaching them how to have integrity, to be decent, to pray, and to study the Bible so they really understand it and can live by it. Many people "play church" because it sounds good as part of a kid's credentials or looks good printed on a program, in a yearbook, or on a resume. We also often lead teens to believe that money and influence and material things are the most important aspects of life. Many wealthy people are the most miserable people in the world because their hearts are empty. They have huge, beautiful homes, fancy all-terrain vehicles, and belong to the country clubs, but they are missing the troop of loyal friends and neighbors, strong family relationships, and Christian love that are really worth living for.

Two sayings I have always held close to heart are:

1) If you don't feel close to God, guess who moved?
and
2) If Jesus had a refrigerator, He would keep your picture on it.

A mother can't really carry spina bifida or any handicap alone. A couple can't either nor a family nor a community nor even a gigantic health care team. It will destroy the child, you, and everyone you love and care about if you don't let God row the boat with you. If you do take God as your partner, you can take that kid with the disability and turn that child into a hero.

If you allow God to lead you, He will bring along His angels. Everyone's angels are different. He has a whole host of them: your mom, dad, sister, brother, sister-in-law, brother-in-law, uncles, aunts, cousins, friends, preacher, neighbor, doctors, nurses, and cook . . . so many angels in so many places. You might not find them in church. Christians don't live in church; some don't even go. Most do, but some had a negative experience in church, and you might find them at the convenience store, dry cleaners, or the insurance office. Look for them; they are all around you.

As Cody's parents, we weren't afraid one bit of extreme sports like zip lining or riding four-wheelers or power sports. Our only fear was his not getting the most out of life. The recipe is stepping out on faith, holding friends and family close, making as little as possible of the bad times, and building self-confidence, then inspiring others so life has purpose. To do that, you have to use the muscles that work and view the disability as just a little inconvenience. You can't be afraid of tough. It's all tough; you just have to be tougher.

Raising handicapped kids, any kids, truly is tough, and you will make mistakes. Be honest with your child and learn to forgive yourself. If your life becomes guilt ridden, depression will consume you, and you will become very non-productive. That kind of shutdown wastes precious, valuable time. The best course for the child and the family is to follow what Henri Frederic Amiel said, "Learn to be what you are, and learn to resign with a good grace all that you are not."[19]

People often ask if I was ever angry about the spina bifida that caused things like a three-year disaster with a leg infection. Mostly, I was just sad. For Cody, for all of the family, it was like planning a trip to Disney World and being rerouted to the local zoo. We tried to keep things light, saw some interesting sights, and made the most of it, but in the back of our minds, we were always aware that it wasn't Disney World. Some things are just not okay, not ever.

Still, no matter what, we kept hope in our hearts. We are so grateful for our blessings of Cody's accomplishments, the wonderful friends we have met, even among disaster, and the faith that is always a candle to light our way through the darkness.

Those three years had taken their toll on Cody and all of us, but I ran across an old song. With that song in our hearts, we moved past the pity party and the horror of that time in our lives. The words to the old hymn that finally rescued us are these:

I don't know about tomorrow, I just live from day to day;
I don't borrow from its sunshine, For its skies may turn to gray;
I don't worry o'er the future, For I know what Jesus said,
And today I'll walk beside Him, For He knows what is ahead.
Every step is getting brighter, As the golden stairs I climb;
Every burden's getting lighter, Every cloud is silver lined;
There the sun is always shining, There no tear will dim the eye;
At the ending of the rainbow, Where the mountains touch the sky.
I don't know about tomorrow, It may bring me poverty;
But the one who feeds the sparrow, Is the one who stands by me;
And the path that be my portion, May be through the flame or flood;
But His presence goes before me, And I'm covered with His blood.
Many things about tomorrow, I don't seem to understand;
But I know who holds tomorrow, And I know who holds my hand.

Ira Stamphill, copyright 1950[20]

Cody's future, like that of anyone else, is uncharted waters. God alone is privileged to know what is coming. I hope for the best. I hope to take it as it comes and not try to reach too far and take on too much. I only know if you want to really give your kids something valuable, give them the words of an anonymous author who said:

DON'T QUIT

When things go wrong, as they sometimes will,
When the road you're trudging seems all up hill,
When the funds are low and the debts are high,
And you want to smile but you have to sigh,
When care is pressing you down a bit,

Rest if you must, but don't you quit.
Life is strange with its twists and turns,
As everyone of us sometimes learns,
And many a failure turns about,
When he might have won had he stuck it out.
Don't give up though the pace seems slow,
You may succeed with another blow.
Success is failure turned inside out–
The silver tint of the clouds of doubt.
And you never can tell how close you are,
It may be near when it seems so far,
So stick to the fight when you're hardest hit,
It's when things seem worst,
That you must not quit!

CHAPTER 9

Our Hero

IF I CAN STOP ONE HEART FROM BREAKING,
I SHALL NOT LIVE IN VAIN;
IF I CAN EASE ONE LIFE THE ACHING,
OR COOL ONE PAIN,
OR HELP ONE FAINTING ROBIN
UNTO HIS NEST AGAIN,
I SHALL NOT LIVE IN VAIN.

Emily Dickinson[21]

Handicapped individuals have a diverse road to travel, not only cultural but also physical. A disabled person will only do well by looking at the adversity as opportunity, at pity and belittling as ignorance, and at avoidance as a lack of understanding. My advice is to live by the golden rule. Treat other people the way you would like to be treated, not necessarily the way they treat you. Return kindness for meanness—hope in the place of despair. Soon ignorance turns to understanding, and those who avoided dealing with the handicap develop compassion and are inspired to exchange avoidance for assistance.

If you are lured into a fight, the ignorance goes on. That is exactly what hecklers want. That will only lower you to the level of the heckler. Instead, conduct yourself with integrity, and like anyone else, you will gain respect.

Don't look for easy days. A few will sneak in, but being productive for anyone, disabled or not, takes vision followed by hard work. I hear kids saying today, "That's hard," as if it were some kind of deadly disease, so they run. When you meet up with tasks that are hard, lower your torso and butt into them head on. The fact is, most people with a disability have to work twice as hard to do half as well as able-bodied people, but it can be done.

Actually, while most "get-rich-quick" schemes are failures, some greatness occurs by accident. A fisherman in the north goes out in the cold every morning and twists his boots to dump ice out of them. The thought occurs to him that people could benefit from that action. He acts on it, and the twist and dump ice tray is born. Someone else tries to invent a new glue and sticks paper everywhere. Forget glue, the Post-it Notes come into being. All these people did was take advantage of the opportunity that presented itself (not to discount the brilliance of doing that). It just shows that we all have abilities. There are opportunities everywhere waiting to be developed. The idea person is just as important as the engineer is. Reach out to others and a team will form. Maybe you have to roll instead of walk. So what? One of Cody's mottos is: "Just do it!"

Statistics show that 1/3 of handicapped individuals drive, even though they only have problems below the waist. Why is that? Hand controls are available in various affordable forms and disabled people driving one-handedly are no different from those people putting on make-up or talking on cell phones while behind the wheel.

Only 50 percent of handicapped people work. The government will send them a guaranteed check for $500 per month, but if they go to work, it stops. Many disabled who work are at menial, part-time jobs with variable hours. So instead, they take the sure money and live in poverty. It will take the continuing efforts and successes of disabled citizens and their supporters to create the needed changes. The *Americans with Disabilities Act* passed in 1990 was a great start. Since that act was put into law, ramps, elevators, and automatic doors are popping up everywhere. Suddenly, handicapped people are able to have experiences in places they never dared to go before.

It would be unrealistic and cruel to pretend that people with disabilities do not have them. Doing that would replace achievable goals with sure failure. A super place for advocates to land is between disabled and able, at "enable." A few times Cody was prevented from participating in activities because of lack of access for wheelchairs. When he was little, we carried him over, under, and around obstacles, but when he reached 5'7" and over 200 pounds that was no longer possible. There were times we had to miss entering a building because of roadblocks like two steps and a narrow passageway. However, he hasn't missed much. We usually found a way. Angels helped us. Now we are trying to help others. People-to-people is God's plan.

Cody is a graduating senior now with a 3.0 GPA. He is headed to college to play wheelchair basketball and major in radio/TV broadcasting. He has an able-bodied girlfriend. She is a junior at the same high school, has a 3.7 GPA, and plans to join him at college when she graduates and wants to major in occupational therapy. Cody announces all of the baseball games for his high school, some of the basketball games, and has "Cody's Corner," a website for sports updates. He also has a spot on the sidelines at the Friday night football games to interview a person of his choice on the radio. All of the football, baseball, basketball, soccer, and track coaches at his high school have been wonderful to Cody and recognize his abilities instead of shunning him because of his handicap. They are a great group of people.

Last year when the football dynasty at his school was in danger of crumbling because of three straight losses (the most consecutive losses in many years), the coaches asked Cody to come talk to the football players during their Friday afternoon meeting.

The following is Cody's speech, exactly as he delivered it to the football players:

Hi guys! I want you to know, 'A hero is a man who does what he can' [22] and from where I sit, all of you look like heroes to me. Make no mistake about it; at our high school, pride is not just a phrase or expression. It is a living, breathing thing! I know it seems like the whole town is down on you now, but when y'all are back, the fans will be back too. This town needs our team's pride, and it needs to be restored at the game tonight. We all want to look for an excuse when things aren't going well and some place to put blame. It's the plays the coaches call—nice try, but all the plays are designed to work with the right execution—We have too much pressure on us—We're too tired—The field's too wet—People expect too much—A barrel full of excuses. I know; I was born with a barrel full of excuses. I wasn't given the ability to walk or run—Thank God for fast-rollin' toxic green wheelchairs, or I wouldn't even be able to handle this school with all of those dang T-buildings. But my Mom has a sign in her office that reads, 'This is Not Whine Country' and my family enforces that. I have had fifteen surgeries, eight stress fractures, and years and years of hospitalizations and IV's and CT scans and therapies. A lot of people said I would never be able to do much, but I adopted a saying of Henry Ford's, the creator of the Found on the Road Dead cars. 'There isn't a person alive who can't do more than he thinks he can.' I didn't want to give up. I wanted to play sports. Even some of the people closest to me said, 'How in the world is he going to do that?' My family said, 'We don't know, first time me, first time you!' So I determined I wanted to be on the high school track team, and the teachers, coaches, and team members were all amazed. Coach M., the adaptive PE coach, started watching films and making a plan. The first time I went to a high school track meet, I sat in the pit in my wheelchair and threw the shot put and discus a few feet in front of me. All the able-bodied athletes just stared. My encouragers said, 'Well, now we have something to build on!' Being in a wheelchair doesn't mean you're stupid. That was just a real nice way of saying, 'That sucked.'

Guys, I had no competition and everyone stared, but I didn't let that get me down. I just remembered what Will Rogers said, 'Everybody is ignorant, only on different subjects!' So we made a plan and executed it, and before the season was over I was at the state track meet, breaking state records, and the quote from the main judge when I threw the shot was, 'God Amighty!' Before another year had passed, I went to the state track meet accompanied by two of our track coaches this time, broke the records from the year before, and went on to the Wheelchair Sports, USA, Jr. National Meet in Connecticut. What did my family tell me? 'Whatever you do, we love you and we are proud of you. None of that changes the fact that we did not come here to watch you throw the thing right in front of your feet.' So I broke not one, but two national records. Now I have been invited to go to a World Competition in Australia in 2004, and I hope to be part of the Paralympics in 2008 in Beijing, China. The majority of people couldn't believe I could do power sports because I'm in a wheelchair, but it doesn't matter what they believe, it only matters what I believe, and I believe I can travel to the other side of the world and bring home the gold! You have a great advantage. You have each other and coaches who give up their lives for you (If you don't believe it, go ask their wives.) and the best conditioning coach and equipment in America. If anything is missing, it is believing you are the best! Football games are not won by putting the plays in the right sequence, but by players who put their hearts into the plays. What if, instead of blaming Coach D.S. or A. or S. or leadership or whining about not being as fast as last year's team or the running backs that have already graduated or your shoes are too tight or your uniforms are the wrong color, you make a decision to reach way down inside of yourself and find what it is that you can really do to add to this team?

WINNING IS NEVER ABOUT TALENT AND ABILITY. IN FOOTBALL OR ANYTHING ELSE IN LIFE, IT IS ALWAYS ABOUT DETERMINATION AND PERSEVERANCE.

Remember, it isn't the play calling causing the losses, it's the way we play the calls. What if our heads and hearts are somewhere else besides the stadium on Friday night? Come on, guys. It's just for three hours! A man named George Eliot said, 'It is never too late to be what you might have been.' And another said, 'Start by doing what is necessary, then what is possible, and suddenly you are doing the impossible.' And a third man said, 'It's a funny thing about life, if you refuse to accept anything but the best, you usually get it.' The fourth said, 'Act as if it were impossible to fail.'[22]

Believe me, I know some people can say being in a wheelchair is not that bad, because they are not in one, and it's easy to say y'all are not trying, because they are not the ones out there sweating blood. Well, do this; put your heart into the game and the rest of you will go with it. Who is this team anyway? I don't know, but I know who they are not. They are not the LSU Tigers or the Dallas Cowboys. They are just kids like us who are coming to our stadium to put the butt whoop on our team, because that's what the other teams from their district did. Well, we have a little surprise for them. Let them do their best; our best is better. So you lost three in a row . . . so what? We're not hurt. We're just a little wounded and stunned—shake it off! Think of the Eagles song and GET OVER IT![23] Don't whine or complain or place blame. What's done is done and it cannot be undone. We are all in this together. Now you have a new job! Let's pull together and show our town and our state and everybody else what football pride is all about! There are seniors on this team that this season is their last dance—They won't get another chance to be a high school football hero—I'm a guy who can only dream of that; you are the guys who can actually be one!

Believe me, you can make a difference! I'm asking you to win this football game and all the rest of this season's games for all of us guys on the sidelines who can only be winning fans. For all of your families who love you and have taken the time to encourage you and haul your butts to hundreds of practices since you were a little kid, for this coaching staff who stays up at night and watches football films instead of being with their families, for the band and all those pretty girls in the cheerleading squad and raiders and pep squad that cheer you on every week, for each other so team pride will really shine, and for the loyal fans who love to say, Who let the dogs out? . . . tonight, when the announcer says, 'Ladies and gentlemen, your team is approaching from the east' . . . make them whisper all over the stadium. 'There is something different about their walk tonight.' If your job is to block a certain player, flatten him before he ever leaves the line of scrimmage. If your job is to catch a pass, grab that ball like it has a million dollars taped to the underside of it. Whatever it takes, do your job!

Now, stand up. . . . Don't ever take for granted that you have the ability to do that.

Let's make a pact . . . tonight when it's all said and done and the final whistle is blown . . . make sure that our opponents will forever remember the 2002 season and the night they played this team! I want to leave you with a quote from the Holy Bible:

This is from Isaiah: 'But they that wait upon the Lord will renew their strength; they shall mount up with wings as eagles; they shall run, and not be weary; they shall walk, and not faint.'[24]

Thanks for listening, and God bless you!

When he was finished, they said you could have heard a pin drop and that continued throughout the meal that night. Cody and that speech have become famous in our town. The team won all the rest of their games that season, all of the playoff games, and went to the Superdome to the state high school football championship. At the door of the Superdome the security guy said, "Son, you can't come in here in that wheelchair without a pass."

About that time, one of the coaches walked up, got behind the wheelchair, and started pushing. He told security, "If you don't mind, our team member will go in with us. If you have a problem with that, the head coach will be here in a minute, and you can discuss it with him." Needless to say, he let them pass. It was hard to imagine the hero for those buffed-up football champions, so loved by the fans, was a high school junior in a wheelchair.

Cody was also one of the Governor's selected heroes. He went to the Governor's mansion, along with the other seven selected, and ate lunch with him. They all took their picture together and then had a wonderful banquet that night.

Being a hero is not always easy, and it is not always fun. Cody learned that lesson last Christmas. Now every Christmas I pick a family project that allows our kids to help children that live in less fortunate circumstances than they do, in the hope that they will learn to live by Christian principles. We hope doing that has helped them to learn about the love and the blessings that they can receive from helping other people.

Last Christmas I felt that the right thing for everyone concerned was to share some joy with a child who also has spina bifida. Not just any spina bifida child, but a twelve-year-old boy who lives nearby. He and his dad live alone in a small apartment. His dad, now in his 30s, was hit by a car when he was a junior in high school and came close to death. He now walks with a distinct limp, using a walking cane to sturdy himself. The supplies that are required to care for a child with a disability are very expensive; our family is certainly aware of that. The father and son team, while sharing a great love for each other, had fallen on hard times. I wanted to help them. I wanted all of us to help them.

After soliciting assistance from Special Children's Services' staff, asking them to ensure that we would not embarrass the boy or his father, asking them to find out their sizes and address, and asking them to arrange a time for our visit with them, everything was set. We had seen them at a few football games, and the child was starting to compete in local wheelchair sports activities, but we did not know them well. I took Abby and Cody shopping with me, and we bought some clothes and toys. We asked Ma to donate a fried turkey and a pan of cornbread dressing (her specialties), which she most graciously did. All four of us were actually excited about following through with our Christmas surprise.

Christmas morning arrived, and we set out to deliver the gifts and food to our friends. As fate would have it, we got our wires crossed. When we arrived at their apartment, they were not there and the door was locked. I was afraid that we were not at the right place and decided to see if we could locate someone to ask. About that time, a beautiful young lady was coming down the stairs from the upper level of apartments. She had a small girl on each side of her. Both of the girls had gorgeous blonde curls, and they were very neatly dressed. Each girl and the mom were carrying packages with pretty wrapping. All three of them were interacting happily with one another, and the two girls were giggling.

I stopped the young lady and asked her if she knew the family we had come to visit. Her voice was audible, but we could not understand her response. We realized from her speech that she was deaf. It was obvious that Cody was deeply moved. We decided to go home and return in a couple of hours to try to deliver our treasures again. We left a note on the door, hoping that it was the right apartment and that the dad would call us. About an hour later, he did just that. We put our lunch on hold and headed back to their home. Paul, Abby, and I talked and sang Christmas carols while Cody remained silent. That was so unusual for him that it troubled me. He was obviously still stunned by the deaf lady and her children.

When we arrived the second time, the dad met us at the door. I am not sure any of us were really prepared for what we saw when we entered that apartment. There they were, father and son, alone on Christmas day in that tiny living room. The room was modestly furnished but clean, and a Bible lay on the coffee table. It was dark because the electricity bill was hard to pay. It was cold and they were wearing their jackets for the same reason. There was no food, no tree, and no presents. Just a doting, disabled father and his son, a boy in a rickety wheelchair. There was no celebration there, but no complaining either. They were just glad to have each other, shelter, and their jackets. All of my family learned something about being thankful that day. We all enjoyed our visit, and the dad and son were both so appreciative of our efforts. We found out that morning that Christmas truly is about love.

A small measure of humor was added to that experience when we loaded into the car and headed home to enjoy our own Christmas lunch. Before anyone else could say a word, Cody immediately unloaded his thoughts on the experience, "Mom, I know you have spent the entire week, especially this morning, trying to teach us a valuable lesson about hardship and sharing what we have with others, and you have, and I appreciate it. Really, I do. But between those guys and the deaf mother with the two little girls, I have about seen all the sadness I can take for one morning. It's Christmas. Do you think we could go home and get happy now, please? Not to be selfish or anything." We all had a laugh. Finding humor to offset sadness was something with which we had plenty of experience.

My reply was, "Sure, Son. As long as you promise to help the needy when you can." He and Abby promised to do that, so we went home and shared a lovely Christmas together.

Cody also made All District Choir, All State Choir, and National Honor Choir. The choir director at the high school, Gerg Nedo, and his wife, who teaches voice and sings beautifully, have been wonderful to Cody. They have helped him to capture many fine opportunities in music, both in school and church, and have become like family to us.

Cody's honors and our adventures have taken him to many places. We flew to New York for National Honor Choir, spent a week in the Roosevelt Hotel, and flew home through the worst snowstorm in 100 years. We went back with his high school choir to sing in Carnegie

Hall on Easter Sunday under the direction of the well-known John Rutter. Planes, trains, subways, broken elevators, none of that stopped us. If you think a big city like New York is handicapped accessible, think again. People with disabilities must be determined. We persevered and saw everything. We even had adventures the other kids missed. We went through a few dark tunnels, took some $25 cab rides, and even managed to take a few rides on the subway. We rode a couple of golf carts across airplane runways in 8-degree weather holding the wheelchair in our laps. He even had a better seat than most at the Broadway shows.

Cody never lost his sense of humor. One memory he created was on the night the choir ate at the Manhattan Chili Company. The area reserved was upstairs. Cody and I were told to go next door to David Letterman's studio, and they would take us up on an elevator. There would be a hall that connected to the Chili Company. When we went in, there was a man sitting at a desk across from the elevator. Cody rolled up to the desk and the man asked, "May I help you?"

Cody replied, "Yes, I am here for my appointment with Mr. Letterman." My chin dropped to the floor.

The guard said, "Son, Mr. Letterman is out of town this week."

Cody came back with, "Okay, then I guess you can take us up to the second floor of the Chili Company to join our party." The guard chuckled. I just rolled my eyes. He entertained all the kids at dinner that night with that story. I am not sure if he would have gotten to meet Mr. Letterman if he had been there or not, but I know keeping things light makes everything that's difficult easier to tolerate.

Our adventures took us to Artist's Point in Yellowstone, on a float trip down the Snake River in Wyoming, to the Grand Canyon, to Oak Creek Canyon, and through the Indian Reservation in Mesa, Arizona, over the Cumberland Gap, to Abraham Lincoln's boyhood home in Kentucky, to Boston, on to Plymouth Rock, and to the chocolate factory in Hershey, Pennsylvania. We drove on to Gettysburg to stand among the graves of the brave men and boys who died in battle there and view the monument erected to honor the only woman who perished by a stray bullet through her kitchen window as she was baking bread. We stood there in that beautiful cemetery, listened to the guide give an account of Abraham Lincoln's famous address, and tell of the history of Gettysburg and the Civil War. Paul and Cody, both with a great love for history, were greatly moved. We also traveled to Florida several times, to Destin beaches, to Shell Island, and on Disney's Big Red Boat to the Bahamas. We've conquered Disney World, MGM, Epcot, and Sea World.

We rode the Amtrak train to New York from Meridian, Mississippi, twenty-six hours each way with Cody's high school choir. The handicapped seat was the last one on the train, and his wheelchair was too wide to get down the aisle. So other than the bathroom trips, he sat in one seat for twenty-six hours each way. He never complained. We played cards and told jokes, the girls and guys took turns coming back to where he was visiting and bringing him food. I said, "Son, I am so sorry you had to sit in that one seat all of that time."

"That's okay, Mom, I am used to sitting. I got to hear everyone's CD's, see Washington from the train, and got to know the kids better."

Does he ever get depressed? Not much because he has learned well how to take what life hands him, add faith, and make good on it. When we took him to an extreme sports camp for the physically challenged a couple of years ago, we stood in line while kid after kid, along with a parent or caretaker, handed the nurse a gallon bag of medicines and almost every one had at least one anti-depressant to take daily. When it was Cody's turn, while looking down, the nurse asked, "What meds is Cody on?"

"None."

She asked twice, "Did you say none?"

Both times I just said, "None." She was stunned.

I finally instructed her, "You can give him a multi-vitamin if you want to. Tylenol if he has a headache, something like that."

Later on Cody asked, "Why don't I take all those meds like the other kids?"

"Oh, I figure if you have to take twenty pills a day you won't have enough time to have fun." We laughed. He had fun on that trip zip lining off a 50-foot tower, kayaking in white water, and playing wheelchair basketball with the camp counselors.

The truth is, except for not walking, the shunt, and an occasional kidney infection, he is very healthy. I believe exercise and sports activities have made him that way. In dealing with Cody's problems, my being a nurse was both a curse and a blessing. The curse was that my knowledge of what could happen caused me to worry more than others and to lose more sleep. The blessing was that I knew if tiny premature babies wouldn't break, Cody wouldn't either. So I told him as soon as he could understand what I meant, "Cody, anything you cannot do is fine with us, but we are going to try it all. We are not going to whine about having spina bifida nor sit around waiting for a spot to open up in a convalescent home." So we did try to do as much as possible.

What is life like for kids with a disability? Lots of doctor's visits with hundreds of hours of waiting, lots of surgeries, x-rays, scans, years of physical therapy working their way through lots of different appliances, annual series of testing like kidney testing that includes ultrasound of the kidneys, triple renal function tests, and IVP, 1 to 2 hours for each test, and they all require IV's, dye, and lying perfectly still for an hour at a time. Daily these kids are battling braces or crutches or wheelchairs, which require constant maintenance for flat tires or spokes that are broken or cushions that wear out. They are constantly outgrowing their braces so they have to go to the doctor and get a prescription, go to the brace place and have a mold made to make the braces, go back for a final fitting, and then go back to the doctor to see how well the braces are working. In between all of this, they try to go to school and have a little fun.

So many times Cody would be the only wheelchair kid in a crowd of 200 students in the All-State Choir or 400 kids in National Honor Choir or 90,000 people at the college football games. Cody hopes to help change that by inspiring wheelchair kids who are able to do so to get out and fulfill their potential so they will have better, healthier, fuller, more productive lives.

As parents, it was tough. We had to work at keeping the family solid. At times, we had to work opposite shifts. We took turns at being depressed. There were issues we disagreed on. There were times we were so scared and sad that we couldn't even look at each other, much less express our feelings. Really, Dr. J. was right, statistics show that somewhere between 85–90 percent of couples who have handicapped children experience a dissolution of their marriage. What statistics do *not* show is the portion of those couples who fall into the realm of the 40–50 percent who split anyway.

It all goes back to basics, starting with your selection of a spouse and what qualities he or she possesses. It is one of the most important decisions a person will ever make. Added to that is how serious you are about your commitment. If your relationship is based on looks, popularity, finances, pity, or a sense of obligation instead of love, respect, admiration, and communication, then failure is a strong possibility. After all, it is best said in the quote,

"Life is the sum of all of your choices."[25]

Raising and caring for a disabled child are extremely difficult, and a marriage will need to be on solid ground plus strive for growth and change in the same direction for both people to survive.

It has been work, but we hung on. God helped us. We just made the most of the good times and as little as possible of the bad. We focused on helping Cody to develop his abilities and to learn to encourage others. We always tried to be open and honest and respect Cody's feelings and each other's feelings. We weren't perfect, just determined. We all used the muscles that worked, including our heart muscles. We took our theme from an old song:

Love lifted me,
Love lifted me,
When nothing else would do,
Love lifted me.[26]

The main thing we learned, as the parents of a spina bifida child and an adopted child, is that being a family doesn't have anything to do with how children look, what their abilities are, or even if they are flesh and blood. It only has to do with having enough love in your heart to carry children through whatever they face growing up.

What do I say about being his mother? I have come to believe that it is the main reason for my life. He has taken Paul, Abby, Ma, Cheryl, me, and the rest of our family and friends on a great adventure, and he isn't through. He says he will be a great sports announcer one day, and he fully intends to marry and have children. I believe he will. I know this; if I hadn't had the privilege of raising him, I wouldn't have known about the world wide web of handicapped people and how important they are, how wonderful they are. If we hadn't faced all the hardships in his life's course, I wouldn't know about the miracles that come from stepping out on faith. If you never experience those kinds of problems and survive by praying your way through them, you don't know that God can solve them. He might let you get way back in a dark corner first, but He will show up!

As parents, we need to be as close to 100 percent every day that we can be. As the parents of a child with a disability, we almost needed to be 200 percent because of the added issues at school, continuous medical care, stairs, ramps, and elevators—a list that never ends. One of the most difficult things for me is control. Because of that, most of the time, I would neither ask for nor accept help. That was a big mistake. You wear out more quickly. I always thought I was the only one who could ask the right questions or give the right reports. Again, it's one of those Oscar Mayer things of "B-O-L-O-G-N-A." God puts people in your path when you need them. For goodness sake and for your health, let them help you. I had an ever-present concern that I would be impos-ing on people. Most of the time that was silly; they wanted to help. It's just that my personality is such that I would wind up trying to help the people who came to help us. Don't do that. Let people help you, and it will enhance the child's life and the lives of the whole family.

One day last fall Cody told me that he wanted to go to a college ballgame, 200 miles away, and he wanted just the two of us to go. I said, "Why? You usually want just you and Dad to go to those games."

"Well, you and I just never have any quality time together."

My astonished response was, "What do you mean? We are always together."

"Yeah, in the doctor's office." He was right. We had spent hun-dreds of hours in waiting rooms, but that is not real quality time. I was still a little surprised at his request, but I agreed.

We decided to pack our tailgating supplies, leave early A.M., and drive back after the game. He seemed excited. We had only gone 20 of the 200 miles when he turned toward me and said, "Mom, I want to talk to you about something I don't want to discuss with anyone else."

My heart fell. I took a deep breath, "Okay, Son. Tell me."

"I woke up one day about two weeks ago and realized that I don't know anyone with spina bifida that is over thirty-five years old." I felt that old familiar lump rise in my throat, and I felt sick.

I quickly told him, "But Cody, there are people with spina bifida who are 40, 50."

He stopped me mid-sentence. " Mom, before you go any further, let me say this. I am in a world-wide web of wheelchair sports now, and none of the people I have met with spina bifida are over thirty-five years old."

I swallowed hard and verbalized this through tears, "Son, I have never lied to you before and I am not going to start now. There are *not* tons of people with spina bifida over thirty-five years old, but I would rather have thirty-five years of wonderful than 150 years of doing nothing. How ever long any of us live, we have been blessed enough to do more and see more and be friends with more fabulous people than most people could do in ten lifetimes. From where I stand in my job, every year I see 5-year-olds die and 3-month-olds die and newborns that should be fine but won't breathe no matter how hard we try to save them. If you try to figure all of that out, you will be crazy, and you still won't know the answers. You will be better off to trust God and His wisdom. The real secret to life is to live as if you are going to live forever, and at the same time, as though today were your last day. If you can do that, you will be okay. Besides, someone may invent a plastic kidney any day now that will save all of you."

He said, " You are right, Mom. Thanks for talking to me about it."

"Sure, Pal. I hope you will always feel comfortable talking to me about anything that is bothering you." I was glad but I was also sad. Sad that my sixteen-year-old son had to have thoughts of death, but glad he was mature enough to have a conversation about it.

Whatever the rest of life is, Cody is our hero. I don't pretend his life is not difficult and challenging, but it is so exciting and rewarding too. Wherever the roller coaster ride takes him from now on, we will be there with him. After that, there's Heaven. I hope when we get to Heaven that we won't remember what spina bifida or any other disability was.

Cody plays basketball for a high school team called the Rollin' Razorbacks, and they were playing a tournament in a different state when I met a nice lady whose fifteen-year-old son played on the opposing team. I asked her if he had spina bifida and this is what she said,

"No, when he was thirteen a four-wheeler accident left him paralyzed from the waist down. I was pregnant, suffered from high blood pressure and toxemia. At delivery, I had a cardio-pulmonary arrest, and they had to do a tracheotomy on me. I went into a coma, and when I woke up, my baby was already five months old. I guess the stress of everything had just been too much for me. Now I am trying to bounce back and help all of my children, especially the one in the wheelchair, to have full lives." I told her about wheelchair sports other than basketball, about praying through one crisis at a time, and that Cody and I would help her and the child as much as we could from three states away. Honestly, those are the kind of tragic stories I am glad we won't be hearing in Heaven.

As I knew he would, Cody vowed to help that child. His leadership ability, maturity, and selflessness are amazing. He always has a smile and a kind word, a word of encouragement for others. He keeps you laughing. It seems like he would need somebody to make *him* laugh. He has this saying that sums up his philosophy about life and it is, "I'll do my best and God will do the rest." He truly is my hero.

CHAPTER 10

The Finish That Goes On

If God came in and said, "I want you to be happy for the rest of your life," what would you do? What do you think a handicapped child would do? Get rid of the handicap? You might be surprised.

MAY THE TIRE TRACKS THAT I LEAVE,
HELP THEM TO BELIEVE,
AND ALL WHO COME BEHIND ME
FIND ME FAITHFUL.

Cody

Cody's footprints are not footprints at all, but rather tire tracks, wheelchair tire tracks, because that is what he was given, what we were given. Many would say, "It's not enough. It's not all that was coming to him."

You can hold with that theory, but I prefer to side with my son who told me at one of the low points for me, "Mom, I wouldn't take anything for being in this wheelchair."

When I regained my composure I asked, "Why is that, Son?"

"Because if I had been a regular kid I don't think I could have inspired anyone, but from this wheelchair people tell me every day what an inspiration I am to them. So I am okay with it." There was a tremendous amount of healing for me in hearing him say that. What a kid! He has so much hope in his heart.

I told him, "I am really proud of you, Son. If you can be comfortable with who you are, then you have come a long way toward maturity that many adults never reach."

On a Sunday morning, not long ago, Cody opened the service at church by playing "Amazing Grace" on his violin, and there was hardly a dry eye in the congregation. The song seemed so fitting because it is God's grace that has seen us to this point in life, and his seventeen years have all been amazing, period. We intend to press on, and I expect great accomplishments in the future, perhaps more exceptional than Cody or any of us can imagine.

You see, Cody and I have discovered along this incredible journey that the race does not go to the swift, but to the persistent. The tortoise was right. It does not matter if you can walk or are bound to a wheelchair, plain or pretty or handsome, short or tall, fat or thin, bright or basic. Even if you are three French fries short of a Happy Meal, God knows the "value of one," and you *can* make a difference if you try.

I find myself dreading again, only this time it is sending him to college, but pride overshadows sadness. Many said he would not be able to do much in the beginning. Now they are astonished. I hope Cody knows my life has been so much more because of him. I now leave him and you with this poem:

THE FUTURE

Take me along, Son, wherever you go;
I'll try to keep up and not go too slow.

In your head and that wheelchair, the wheels turn so fast;
As you seek out adventure, making memories that will last.

Memories we will lean on when things get real tough;
We learned how to do that, in the past, when things were rough.

Keep building your Faith, Pal;
Remember always to pray.

Jesus will surely guide you,
As you trust Him along the way.

Thanks for being the great kid that you are.
Not many people expected a handicapped star.

You took what the Lord gave you, plus Courage, Faith, and Love,
Kept inspiring other people, pleasing God up above.

What a privilege it is to be your Mom;
I look back now and see just how far you have come.

At first they made a long list of things you could not do,
Most of which you accomplished by the time you were two.

You continued to achieve, meeting goal after goal;
I hope that continues until you are old.

Letting you grow up is a hard thing to ask;
Of all the battles we've fought, it is the hardest task.

Independence was the goal we pressed toward; it is still hard to let go,
Even though in the future you will make us proud, I know.

So, dear Son, I find myself encompassed in thought
Of all the joy to our lives you have brought.

And when by others, "I couldn't have done it," I am told,
I reply, "Nonsense, the good outweighs the bad, tenfold."

Now I find myself asking, as you prepare to leave home,
"At least in your heart, Son, please take me along."

I have to cut the cord now, Give you the freedom you deserve;
It just would not be fair to find your parents around every curve.

Take what we taught you; Add more and more good.
Remember to treat others the way God says that you should.

Don't forget where home is; it's *always* there, you must know;
Just whenever possible, please take me with you wherever you go . . .

Love always,
Mom

Through it all, Cody understands that the difference between ordinary and extraordinary people is that little something "extra." *God Bless You All* in whatever struggles you face.

THE END

IN CONCLUSION . . .

There is a vision that Cody and I have for this book, and we summed it up in the following two lines:

May it be an inspiration to all who read it
And a guide to all who need it.

It seems odd that the word "disabled" and the word "child" could ever belong in the same sentence, much less in a child's life, but it happens. Robert Frost explained Cody's life when he wrote in a poem, "Two roads diverged in a wood, and I—I took the one less traveled by, And that has made all the difference."[27]Handicaps by their nature are limiting, and I realize not all disabled children have Cody's potential. But take heart, because while all disabled children cannot do everything, even in the world of activities available to them, they all can do something. As soon as Cody could understand, I told him, "Son, anything you cannot do is fine with us, but we are going to try it all. We will not attend pity parties, and we will set our sights high. When we fall, we will rise and try again." We weren't perfect; we made some mistakes, but we trusted God and always vowed to move onward and upward. It worked out. Cody became a "stand up guy" without the ability to stand.

Whether you have a disabled child in your life or not, look around and you will find one close by. Be encouraging to those families. The journey is difficult, but it may surprise you to know that a very tiny act of thoughtfulness can be such an uplifting experience for that child that he will remember it for all of his life.

I want to share one final thought in closing from an anonymous author:

A hundred years from now it will not matter what my bank account was,
the kind of car I drove, or the type of house I lived in,
but the world may be different because I was important in the life of a child.

RESOURCES

Wheelchair Sports- <u>wsusa@aol.com</u>
Spina Bifida Association- www.sbaa.org

WORKS CITED

[1] Rice, Alice Hegan, *Mrs. Wiggs of the Cabbage Patch,* (1897) Chicago, Religious Publishing Company, Chicago, Illinois.

[2] Von Goethe, Johann, (1749–1832), *Perseverance, Poems, Poems, Poems,* Internet

[3] Powell, Colin, From *First Seargent's Diamond Guidance,* "Bad news does not get better with age." ISG Arthur Van Wyngarden, Internet.

[4] Crosby, Fanny, (1826–1899) *All The Way My Savior Leads Me, The Broadman Hymnal,* Broadman Press, Nashville, Tenn. (1941)

[5] Neibular, Reinhold, *The Serenity Prayer,* (end of a long prayer) (1932)

[6] Hallmark Cards, Inc., (1972) *Hello Sunshine,* Kansas City, Missouri.

[7] Emerson, Ralph Waldo, (1803–1882) Quotes from Ralph Waldo Emerson, Internet

[8] Denver, John, (1990) *I Want to Live,* on I Want to Live (CD) released by RCA.

[9] Lynn (a student representative during a Job Search Workshop) (October, 1998) given to instructor Julie Wilson in Canada.

[10] Dickinson, Emily, (1830–1886) Emily Dickinson Quotes, Internet.

[11] Hallmark Cards, Inc., (1972) *Hello Sunshine,* Kansas City, Missouri.

[12] Alabama, (1989) *Song of the South,* on Southern Star (CD) released by RCA.

[13] Crabb, Gerald, (2002) *Through the Fire,* on A Crabb Collection (CD) released by Family Music Group. (used by permission)

[13] Hoffman, Rev. E.A., (1949) *I Must Tell Jesus, New Songs of Inspiration No. 4,* John T. Benson Publishing Company.

[14] Holy Bible, (King James Version), The Gideons International 1984 edition, Proverbs 16:18.

[15] Davis, Jimmie, and Mitchell, Charles, (1940) *You Are My Sunshine,* Peer International Corporation.

[16] Lightoller, Charles Hebert, (15, April, 1912), 2nd Officer on the Titanic, *Rekindling Memories of the Titanic Tragedy,* Internet.

[17] Commonwealth of Malaysia, "Just because the river is quiet, does not mean the alligators have left."
Internet.

[18] Moore, Clement Clark, *The Night Before Christmas,* poem (1822) Internet.

[19] Amiel, Henri Frederic, (1821–1881) Famous Quotes, Internet.

[20] Stamphill, Ira, (1950) *I Know Who Holds Tomorrow, New Songs Of Inspiration No. 4,* John T. Benson Publishing Company.

[21] Dickinson, Emily, (1830–1886) Emily Dickinson Quotes, Internet.

[22] Rolland, Romain (1966) Quotes from the Columns, Internet.

[22] Haynes, Cyndi, *Change For the Best,* New York, 2000.

[23] Eagles, (1994) *Get Over It,* on Hell Freezes Over (CD) released by Geffen.

[24] Holy Bible (King James Version), The Gideons International, 1984 edition, Isaiah 40:31.

[25] Haynes, Cyndi, *Change For the Best,* New York, 2000.

[26] Smith, Howard E., (1912) *Love Lifted Me,* lyrics by James Rowe, *The Broadman Hymnal,* Broadman Press, Nashville, Tennessee. (1941)

[27] Frost, Robert, (1920) *The Road Not Taken,* The Poetry of Robert Frost (1874–1963), Internet.

Contact author Raina Futrell
at codyandraina@yahoo.com
or order more copies of this book at

TATE PUBLISHING, LLC

127 East Trade Center Terrace
Mustang, Oklahoma 73064

(888) 361 - 9473

Tate Publishing, LLC

www.tatepublishing.com